Cinema Entertainment

Cinema Entertainment

Essays on audiences, films and film-makers

Alan Lovell and Gianluca Sergi

 Open University Press

Open University Press
McGraw-Hill Education
McGraw-Hill House
Shoppenhangers Road
Maidenhead
Berkshire
England
SL6 2QL

email: enquiries@openup.co.uk
world wide web: www.openup.co.uk

and Two Penn Plaza, New York, NY 10121-2289, USA

First published 2009

Mixed Sources
Product group from well-managed
forests and other controlled sources
www.fsc.org Cert no. TT-COC-002769
© 1996 Forest Stewardship Council

A catalogue record of this book is available from the British Library

ISBN-13: 978-0-33-522251-3 (pb) 978-0-33-522252-0 (hb)
ISBN-10: 0-33-522251-X (pb) 0-33-522252-8 (hb)

Library of Congress Cataloging-in-Publication Data
CIP data applied for

Typeset by YHT Ltd, London
Printed in UK by Bell and Bain Ltd, Glasgow.

Fictitious names of companies, products, people, characters and/or data that may be used herein
(in case studies or in examples) are not intended to represent any real individual, company,
product or event.

Contents

Acknowledgements

This was a very difficult book to write. Although this can be said of all books of course, we both felt that in this case we had to really push the boat out to the outer limits of the lake! As a consequence, we have many people to thank for their help and support.

We would like to thank Walter Murch, Dennis Muren, Gary Rydstrom and Randy Thom for their invaluable help and support. We would also like to thank all those who have helped us arrange for the interviews and provided us with very useful material at Industrial Light and Magic, Skywalker Ranch, and Pixar.

We would like to thank all our good friends who have helped us stay sane through the project especially Gill Branston, Jim Kitses, Peter Kramer, and Julian Stringer for their insightful comments. In particular, Gianluca would like to thank Kris Grainger for his support throughout this project, especially at the time of the interviews.

A special thanks to Sophie Styles and Serena Formica whose help as research assistants in the early stages of this project enabled us to form a clearer idea as to the direction of the book. In particular, their energy and enthusiasm for the project were a great encouragement to us and were greatly appreciated.

Our families, as ever, provided us with support and inspiration all the way throughout the writing process. Gianluca would like to thank his family in Italy for their unfailing support. A very special, heartfelt thanks to Cathy (especially for putting up with his absences while doing the interviews!), and children *extraordinaire* Monica and Paolo. He is also very grateful to Avril for all her support.

Alan would like to thank Tessa and Howell for shared viewings and lively discussions.

All photos and illustrations by permission of The Kobal Collection.

We have lost close family members during the writing of this book. We would like to dedicate this book to our families.

Introduction
Cinema as entertainment

What role does entertainment have in our lives? The rapid development of mass media forms such as cinema, radio, comics, television meant that this question was increasingly asked during the twentieth century. It's more accurate to say that it was the role entertainment had in *other* people's lives – the working classes, the bourgeoisie, the masses – that most writers were worried about. At the beginning of the twenty-first century, concerns about the dumbing down of culture, in part, provoked by the emergence of new mass media forms such as the internet and video games, have given the question a contemporary accent. Does the easy availability and increasing presence of entertainment in Western societies mark a decline in the quality of cultural life?

The cinema has been, for much of the time, at the centre of this discussion as this response to the new Batman film, *The Dark Knight*, indicates:

> Britain appears to be gulping down entertainment values wholesale from a Hollywood intent upon mining the profit margin from barbarism. America, for all its manifold strengths, is still a country in which the population can be aroused to a frenzy of condemnation by the sight of Janet Jackson's escaped nipple on the Super Bowl, but views the sight of a bound man being torched to death as all-round family entertainment.[1]

Early film theorists and critics were anxious to detach the cinema from entertainment. They wanted to give it the status of the established art forms. This anxiety about the cinema's cultural status is understandable: any new form is likely to suffer from it. But the uncertainty was heightened by the cinema's strong connections with 'low' forms like vaudeville, funfairs and circuses. Writers like Rudolf Arnheim (*Film as Art*), Bela Balazs (*Theory of the Film*) and Ernest Lindgren (*The Art of the Film*) argued that film belonged with drama, classical music and painting and deserved the same kind of respect.[2] Outside the small world of film enthusiasts, their arguments had little impact. It was only in the 1950s that arguments for cinema as art started to have a wider and more profound impact. The arguments put forward in the journal *Cahiers du Cinéma* at that time had a wide and profound impact, shaping the way the cinema was to be thought about and discussed for the next 50 years. Critics, film-makers, academics and film fans were all influenced by *Cahiers'* arguments.

The foundation of the magazine's position was its analysis and celebration of the work of film directors. A pantheon of directors emerged from its pages. Directors such as Jean Renoir, Roberto Rossellini, Alfred Hitchcock, Howard Hawks and Max Ophuls were championed as artists whose work revealed the true nature of cinema. The *Cahiers* critics went on to claim that films like *La Règle du Jour*, *Voyage to Italy* and *Rear Window* had a formal beauty and thematic profundity that made them the equals of the masterpieces of the modern Western tradition such as *Ulysses*, *The Waste Land* and *Les demoiselles d'Avignon*.

In essence, the *Cahiers* critics maintained that the cinema was an art because great artists worked in it. Directors like Renoir, Rossellini and Hitchcock were the equivalents of James Joyce, Pablo Picasso and T.S. Eliot. From this foundation, a more extensive view of cinema as art emerged. Beginning from the assumption that art was a form of individual expression, its central claims were: (1) the director is the expressive artist in film-making; and (2) film is a visual art so the quality of its images determines a film's expressiveness. This account of the cinema was both influential and liberating. A new canon of great film-makers was established: directors such as Hitchcock and Hawks, whose work had previously been ignored or dismissed as lightweight, were now identified as major figures. New critical concepts supported the canon: '*auteur*' and '*mise en scène*' promised a more sophisticated understanding of how films worked.

At the time, *Cahiers*' position appeared to be a radical one. Its critical judgements certainly were: its support for mavericks and oddballs such as Jerry Lewis, Frank Tashlin and Samuel Fuller was vivid proof of this. Now, with the benefit of hindsight, the conservative frame within which those judgements were enclosed is more obvious. The importance and value of art were taken for granted – the anti-art impulse strongly present in art movements such as Dadaism and Surrealism had little influence. And the distinguishing marks of art – personal expressiveness, thematic depth, formal sophistication – belong to Romanticism.

Cahiers' conservatism meant that important issues were ignored. In this book, we're concerned with one we think is crucial – cinema as entertainment. Despite the success *Cahiers* had in arguing the case for cinema as art, cinema is still more associated with entertainment than art. And with good reason, since the cinema has always been embedded within the world of entertainment. Over its history, it has had close connections with music halls, amusement arcades, best-selling novels, pop music and television. The best-known cinema in the world, Hollywood, invariably describes itself as providing entertainment: audiences, when questioned, regularly say they go to the cinema for entertainment.

In this book, we explore questions that have emerged out of cinema's place in this debate. Our focus is on Hollywood because so much of the discussion about entertainment has concentrated on it. The structure of the book isn't a linear one. Entertainment proved to be an elusive phenomenon, so each chapter discusses it from a different perspective, using different methods: statistical analysis, practical criticism, interviews and critical discussion.

We begin the book by examining whether the most popular films support common assumptions about the nature of entertainment. Our analysis of *The Dark Knight*, in Chapter 2, acts both as a case study and as an opportunity to discuss the nature and effect of sensual pleasure in a film. We go on to consider the achievements of Alfred Hitchcock and Steven Spielberg. Are they best described as entertainers or does the description diminish their achievements? Do film-makers think of themselves as entertainers? We discuss this issue with two film-makers, Walter Murch and Randy Thom, who have been important contributors to some of the most successful Hollywood films of recent years. The book ends with a general discussion of the concept of entertainment.

Figure 1.1 A London premiere for *Gone With the Wind*
(Selznick/MGM/The Kobal Collection)

1 What audiences go for
Elite and mass taste

Fifty-one respondents chose to write about why they went to the cinema and the reasons they give were all variations on entertainment, amusement, relaxation, to be taken out of themselves, to escape the cares of the world and everyday life. But a further 26 mentioned that they valued films as a source of education, inspiration, knowledge.[1]

Films of high quality do occasionally emerge from Hollywood: John Huston's early films were first-rate and Stanley Kubrick promises to be an authentic movie talent if his anger holds out. But such films are infrequent, seldom box-office successes, and never written to formulas. For films of quality proceed not from the demands of a mass audience but from the painful prodding of an artist's conscience. They do not creep along the surface of the skin, but journey deep into the recesses of the soul.[2]

Formulas have value in many different areas of human life. In teaching and learning, tried and tested approaches to a particular subject can be extremely beneficial; in sciences, formulas are the conduit to unlocking complex problems and questions in fields such as mathematics, physics and chemistry; in philosophical thinking, the notion of a formula as a means to reach happiness (or other states of being) has received a great deal of attention; in linguistics, the adoption of established linguistic formulas facilitate the learning of a foreign language.

The need for formulas in communication is a well-known issue in instances where there is a variety of highly specialized and skilled workers working under time and budget constraints. Construction is a typical example, sharing many similarities with cinema. Architects need to make themselves understood to engineers who need to communicate effectively to foremen who need to cascade information down to builders, and so forth.

In the cinema, formulas are used specifically as a means to facilitate communication between film-makers and audiences: directors need to make themselves understood by a variety of other film-makers who have their own specialist languages. Complex choices need communicating to other film-makers in a form that is both quick and effective: the history of film-making is littered with examples of poor interpersonal communication resulting in projects ending up going over budget, over time and nowhere fast. The most common of formulas in this sense is film-makers' use of existing films. A much derided practice among critics (who often laugh at the need to pitch a film to a studio using formulas such as 'it is *Gladiator* meets *The Sixth Sense*') employing previous examples to signify a practice, genre or overall approach to a new project is both logical and necessary find common ground and a shared language with

ent, formulas also have the opposite connotation.
.d film-makers has been that formulas represent the
.y and artistic relevance, as the opening quotation
mulas in films is likened to a sleep of consciousness,
: familiar and the predictable. The use of formulas by
.m being called true artists and relegates them to the
perched on the abyss of insignificance. In the strongest
.nakers using formulas are depicted as downright hacks
positive to this negative is usually thought to be the risk-
roven auteur director who make the search for originality a
.heir film-making.
.s established: individual vs. formulaic. The individual (or the
xpresses a personal world-view. The formulaic is characterized
sporting repetitive storylines that are resolved with unam-
More often than not, this juxtaposition has clear geopolitical
cinema (art) is innovative and risk-taking while Hollywood
.itional and risk averse.

.uick reference, some of the implicit items of conventional wis-
.haracterize not only the cinematic divide: Europe stands for art,
.r pop; Europe for high culture, America for mass entertainment;
.tisanal craft, America for industrial mass production; Europe for
.), Hollywood for studio (box office); European cinema for pain and
.ellort, Hollywood for pleasure and thrills; Europe for the auteur, Hollywood for
the star; Europe for experiment and discovery, Hollywood for formula and
marketing; Europe for the film festival circuit, Hollywood for Oscar night; Europe for the festival hit, Hollywood for the blockbuster.[3]

The debates and views briefly summarized above are of obvious concern to the themes of
this book. Popular entertainment in the cinema and other art forms has often been
defined as the polar opposite to art, in the ways Elsaesser highlights in the above quotation. In particular, the geopolitics of the debate are hardly ever questioned: Hollywood
film-makers are thus juxtaposed to either the 'homeless' independents or the European
film-makers. Increasingly, other 'poles' are being drawn into the debate, especially Asian
cinema, but this hasn't changed the terms of the discussion: Hollywood remains the
motherland of popular entertainment and, as such, the major provider of formulaic film-
making.

Film-makers who make a commitment to their audience a priority often invoke
notions of what the audience 'wants'. Conversely, critics of Hollywood often argue that
mainstream audiences are unwilling or incapable of dealing with anything other than
formula films. However much they are invoked, implicitly or explicitly, audiences remain
a virtually unknown entity in this debate. In order to develop the discussion further we
decided to analyse the nature of the choices audiences make.

more explicit in European cinema because ......

The survey

In order to find out about the nature of the choices film audiences make, we used a sample survey of the top 50 films chosen by elites as best ever and the top 50 films chosen by a mass audience. (See Appendix 1 for an explanation of our methodology.) The questions we wanted answered are:

1   Is there any evidence that audiences prefer a certain 'type' of film? Is there, in other words, a formula that audiences seem to respond to?
2   If the answer is yes, what features characterize it?
3   What about critics? Do their choices show evidence of formulas at work?

The method

The traditional way of answering these questions would be through critical interpretation of a small number of films. Having become increasingly aware of the limitations of this approach, we decided to try to answer them using statistical analysis.[4] Given the limited amount of time and resources at our disposal, a statistical analysis of the kind we have attempted is inevitably fraught with dangers, and we are fully aware of the risks involved in this attempt. However, we believed that the risks were worth taking if our approach helped to advance the discussion.

Two key questions were central for us: how big a sample we should consider and what criteria we should use to select the sample. Since our project is an investigation of the character of cinema entertainment, the tastes of mass audiences are a central concern. We decided that the best starting point for finding about those tastes would be an examination of the US domestic box office. The information about this is relatively rich. Its quality enables us to cross-reference results and refine them by adjusting figures for inflation and by taking account of the number of times films have been re-released.

We thought we'd get a better perspective on the tastes of mass audiences if we could contrast them with the tastes of a different group. Our starting point for this was the *Sight & Sound* poll of the 'best ever' films. The poll, widely recognized as the longest running and most comprehensive of such lists, selects the films that critics and scholars consider the pinnacle of cinematic production over the decades. The scholars who make the choices are mainly university lecturers while the critics come from either film magazines or newspapers and journals whose readers can be expected to have a particular interest in the cinema. It seems fair to describe this group as an 'elite' one. To keep our project a manageable one, we analysed the top 50 films from each list.[5] For mass audiences, this means the 50 films which have attracted the largest audiences over the cinema's history. For elite audiences, this means the 50 films which topped the most recent *Sight & Sound* poll (2002), (available at http://www.bfi.org.uk/sightandsound/topten/poll/critics/html.)

What features did we look for in these films? There have been previous studies, like *The Classical Hollywood Cinema* and Robert McKee's and Syd Field's scriptwriting manuals, which have discussed the existence of formulas in films.[6] They've been most concerned with overall, deep-lying structures. Most Hollywood films may be organized around such structures: what intrigued us is what lies within that structure, the combination of features that determine the particular DNA of any given film. What features, if any, recur in the choices the mass audience or the elite audience make? Is there a pattern (or several?) that can be identified from the data?

Narrative

We chose those features of a film that are the building blocks of its narrative structure. They are the most interchangeable features of a film, open to almost countless permutations and nuance. They provide basic information, such as *when* (timeframe of the story), *where* (location settings), and *who* (status of main character, situation he/she finds him/herself in). We also took into account genre and the scope of the narrative (epic, concern with life and death issues). We extended this by looking at two areas whose discussion in contemporary film scholarship has a direct bearing on our interest in cinema entertainment. The first is the representation of gender, race and (to a lesser extent) class. The second is the development of Hollywood since the 1970s.

Social attitudes

Influenced by Marxism, critics and scholars have suggested that films represent race, gender and class in a way that supports the established power structures of Western societies. We're particularly interested in this position because it often implies that entertainment is used as a disguise for the expression of conservative social attitudes. Simple measures were employed to explore the issue: ones audiences might be aware of without viewing a film two or three times. We looked for films where women/blacks are central characters in the drama. Because of its complexity, the concept of class was more difficult to handle. Financial status was taken as an indicator and we established four main classifications: films where the main character is: (1) struggling or poor; (2) comfortable or wealthy; (3) pitted against a character from the opposite end of the financial strata (e.g. poor vs. rich); and (4) any of the above but his/her financial status is ignored as insignificant to the development of the narrative.

In all four cases, we compared the choices of films made before 1970 with those made after 1970. We did this to see if the social and cultural upheavals of the 1960s had an impact on audience tastes. Were film preferences pre-1970 significantly different from those post-1970?[7]

Hollywood developments

An influential account of the development of modern Hollywood cinema and its audiences is directly relevant to our concern with entertainment. This account claims that, roughly from *Jaws* onwards, Hollywood cinema shifted dramatically towards entertainment and away from art: films became more light and superficial because they were directed at teenagers and family audiences rather than offering adult themes to adult audiences. To test this claim we checked whether the number of post-1975 teenage/family-oriented films had increased substantially, and, conversely, whether the number of adult-oriented films had decreased.

We also explored a number of other issues related to this thesis about the character of

Hollywood films over the past 30 years. A familiar claim is that Hollywood films must have 'happy endings'. How many films do end happily? Is the presence of a well-known/ influential producer or director important for the box office success and/or critical status of a film? How influential is advanced technology such as Computer Generated Imagery and surround sound on audience taste? What kind of sources, adapted or original, do scripts come from? A popular notion about post-1975 films is that their success depends on their origins in an already successful product that pre-exists the film, be it a book, comic book, videogame, or TV series, because this creates a film project that has a built-in audience.

Tables and data variables

Genre

How does genre figure in the choices of our two groups? Are particular genres favoured while others are neglected? In order to answer this question we grouped genres according to three main 'categories': (1) the 'serious' (crime, drama, biography); (2) the 'light' (comedy, romance, musical); and (3) the 'Unreal' (sci-fi, fantasy, animation).[8]

The data shown in Tables 1.1 to 1.3 reveal that the choices of mass audiences are spread equally across films from all three groups. The Elite list, however, heavily favours 'serious' films. Sci-Fi, Fantasy and Animation, the genres which generally have the lowest prestige, are also the least favoured by critics.

Table 1.1 Unreal genres: sci-fi, fantasy and animation

Mass audience	Elite audience
48% (24/50)	12% (6/50)

Table 1.2 Light-hearted genres: comedy, romance, musical

Mass audience	Elite audience
46% (23/50)	28% (14/50)

Table 1.3 Serious genres: crime, drama, biography

Mass audience	Elite audience
40% (20/50)	88% (44/50)

Endings

> I think it would be immoral to present a ready-made solution at the end of a movie. Such a solution would necessarily be forced and, therefore, false ... I haven't found a final solution myself and I would consider myself finished if I had found it. I don't have any certainty or clarity myself; it would be dishonest to give it to the characters of my movies. It is more honest to leave in the viewer a torment that can engender meditation, instead of offering an euphoric solution at any price.[9]

Endings are probably the element most cited when attempts are made to identify Hollywood's 'formula'. The assumption is simple: Hollywood films adopt 'happy end' to minimize the risk of unsettling film audiences. Conversely, art and independent filmmakers choose more open, ambiguous or downright unhappy endings for their films. As Table 1.4 shows, 72 per cent of films in the Mass audience list can be categorized as having a happy ending, so our analysis support this assumption. However, there remains a significant proportion of films (28 per cent, more than 1 in 4) that don't have happy endings. Similarly, the Elite list (Table 1.5) confirms the assumptions in that 66 per cent of films have an ending other than a happy one.

Table 1.4   Endings

Mass audience	Elite audience
Happy: 72% (36/50)	Happy: 34% (17/50)
Other than Happy: 28% (14/50)	Other than Happy: 66% (33/50)

Table 1.5   Ambiguous and/or open ending

Mass audience	Elite audience
Ending: 18% (9/50) as either ambiguous (7) or open (2)	Ending: 24% (12/50) as either ambiguous (9) or open (3)

Closer scrutiny reveals some interesting aspects. The most striking appears when testing the widely agreed belief that Hollywood entertainment, unlike art and independent cinema, presents audiences with a neatly tied resolution, typically the so-called 'Hollywood ending'. Fellini's position, illustrated in the quotation above describes the kind of ending one is likely to find in non-Hollywood films. Consequently, it would be reasonable to expect a difference between the two lists in terms of films that have a well-defined ending, one that resolves most, if not all, of the narrative questions posed by the story. However, the data do not support this view at all. In fact, the two lists show remarkable similarities. As Table 1.5 shows, not only do the two lists have similar percentages of films with either an open ending or an ambiguous ending to the film (18 per cent (9/50) and 24 per cent (12/50) of films in the Elite audience lists, respectively) but the internal division of that figure also indicates remarkable parallels with seven Mass films and nine Elite films that have an ambiguous ending and two Mass films and three Elite films that have an open ending.

In other words, audiences of popular entertainment would appear to be just as willing to reward films without a clear-cut ending than critics are. Conversely, the Elite list also clearly privileges films with a clear resolution.

Star

The importance of stars for audiences is strongly supported by our data. Stars were present in 74 per cent of the Mass audience list. Since we chose to focus only on live action films for this category, 18 per cent of films in the Mass list came under the 'inapplicable' heading, making the star results even more significant (note: this is not so much because we believe that there is not a 'star system' at play in animation, but simply because we believe that star presence is manifested in animated films in a very different way from live action films). The Elite audience also privileges films with a star in them. Over half of the films sampled (52 per cent) show the presence of a star. Table 1.6 shows the full spread of the sample.

Table 1.6 Star presence

Mass audience	Elite audience
Stars: 74% (37/50)	Stars: 52% (26/50)
No Stars: 8% (4/50)	No Stars: 48% (14/50)
Inapplicable: 18% (9/50)	Inapplicable: 0% (0/50)

Source

Hollywood popular cinema, especially post-*Jaws*, has often been accused of relying heavily on existing material believing that audiences will be attracted by a well-known novel/film/comic book, especially one that has received a good deal of publicity. Table 1.7 shows the overall figures for both lists.

Table 1.7 Script source

Mass audience	Elite audience
Original source: 42% (21/50)	Original source: 52% (26/50)
Adapted source: 58% (29/50)	Adapted source: 48% (24/50)

The data only partly confirm this belief. While it is true that the Mass audience list shows a slight preference for adapted films (58 per cent), the majority comes from films released prior to *Jaws*. Table 1.8 shows the data divided by the '*Jaws* watershed'. In the Mass audience list, the films based on original material made after 1974 outnumber those released before *Jaws* by a 2:1 margin (14 films to 7 films). This means that although there was an overwhelming majority of films based on pre-existing material prior to what is understood as the era of the 'package' (74 per cent of films from the pre-1975 sample are adapted) (see Table 1.9), the results were dramatically reversed post-*Jaws* (itself an adapted film, of course) with over 60 per cent of films from the post-1974 sample being from an original screenplay. In short, Mass audiences have preferred more films based on original material figure in the contemporary era than ever before.[10] We haven't included any data from the Elite list here since the sample is not significant given the overwhelming presence of pre-1974 films in the list (see 'Time clusters' on p. 12).[11]

Table 1.8 Mass audience: adapted vs. original source post-*Jaws*

Original: 61% (14/23)	*Adapted*: 39% (9/23)

Table 1.9 Mass audience: adapted vs. original source pre-*Jaws*

Original: 26% (7/27)	*Adapted*: 74% (20/27)

Primary audience addressed

> By far the worst aspect of this cultural imperialism (as the great film critic of the *New Yorker*, the late Pauline Kael, once pointed out) is how *Star Wars* and its clones have infantilised the adult movie audience, transforming the spectator into a child again, overwhelming him with THX sound and ILM spectacle, and leaving no room for aesthetic self-consciousness and critical reflection.[12]

Given the prevalence of 'light entertainment' genres in the Mass audience list we wondered whether this indicated what has been identified as a key feature of contemporary Hollywood, namely audiences prioritizing family-oriented films at the expense of more adult films and themes. As Table 1.10 shows, the picture is far less clear than might be anticipated. In fact, the majority of films in the Mass audience list are adult-oriented films (54 per cent). Results from the Elite audience list are overwhelmingly in favour of adult films with 96 per cent of films in that category. If one result can be drawn here, it isn't so much that Mass audiences prefer family films but that critics have in effect separated the family film from the concept of 'quality'.

Table 1.10 Primary audience

Mass audience	Elite audience
Primarily addressed to family audiences: 46%	Primarily addressed to family audiences: 4%
Primarily addressed to adult audiences: 54%	Primarily addressed to adult audiences: 96%

The picture complicates further when the results are organized in order to analyse possible changes over time. Table 1.11 shows the changes in audience address in both lists using 1975, the year of the release of *Jaws*, as a watershed.

Table 1.11 Primary audience, *Jaws* watershed

Mass audience	Elite audience
Primarily addressed to family audiences: Pre-*Jaws* (11/27): 41% of relative sample Post-*Jaws* (12/23): 52% of relative sample	Primarily addressed to family audiences: Pre-*Jaws* (2/46): 4% of relative sample Post-*Jaws* (0/4): 0% of relative sample
Primarily addressed to adult audiences: Pre-*Jaws* (16/27): 59% of relative sample Post-*Jaws* (11/23): 48% of relative sample	Primarily addressed to adult audiences: Pre-*Jaws* (44/46): 96% of relative sample Post-*Jaws* (4/4): 100% of relative sample

The data would seem to suggest that there is a shift towards family-oriented films but that this is actually rather minimal, just over 10 per cent of the relative samples (i.e. pre- or post-1975). The Elite audience data unequivocally confirm a very strong preference for adult-oriented films in both periods.

Time clusters

We looked to see if there was the prevalence of any particular time (here expressed in decades for the sake of convenience rather than any particular belief in the cohesion of the decade as a sample) in either list. Perhaps unsurprisingly, the films in both lists spread across a rather significant portion of the recent history of film, although there are some significant differences. In the case of the Mass audience list, films are spread rather evenly across the time span they cover. In the case of the Elite audience, however, films are weighted more towards the first half of the century: 68 per cent of films in the list were made before 1960. More remarkably, only 10 per cent of films in the list come from 1970 onwards. For the Elite audience, the last 40 years of film-making in the world have only produced five of the best 50 films of all time, with no films at all post-1983 (*Fanny and Alexander* is the most recent title to appear in the list). An interesting corollary to this is one concerning style. While the Mass list shows the virtual totality of its sample as being in colour (98 per cent), the reverse is true for critics, where 80 per cent of films in the Elite list are in black and white.

Timeframe

The results of the Genre analysis suggested that the taste of the Mass audience allows for a variety of timeframes (i.e. films can be set in the past, present, future or in an unspecified time) more than critics. Our analysis of the timeframe data supports this conclusion. Table 1.12 shows an overwhelming preference in the Elite audience list for films that are set either in the present or past (94 per cent of the sample), with only 6 per cent of films set either in the future or in an unspecified time. Although the Mass audience list shows a similar preference for films set in the present or past (70 per cent), nearly one film in three is either set in the future or in an unspecified time (30 per cent), confirming the impression that the Genre data had generated of a particular bias in the Elite list against films set in the future or in a not better specified 'timeless' land.

Table 1.12 Timeframe

Mass audience	Elite audience
Present: 32% (16/50)	Present: 48% (24/50)
Past: 38% (19/50)	Past: 46% (23/50)
Future & Unspecified: 30% (15/50)	Future & Unspecified: 6% (3/50)

Situation

To pursue this line of investigation further, we looked at the 'situation' that the films' characters had to face in both lists. We divided the sample according to four key situations: ordinary, extraordinary, fantastic/supernatural and other (the latter mostly occupied by animation films).[13] Data from both lists confirm that in the case of both the Mass audience list and the Elite audience list, films with an ordinary setting are in a definite minority, with only 20 per cent of cases falling in this bracket for the Mass audience list and 24 per cent for the Elite audience list. Clustering the 'other-than-ordinary data', the result (respectively 80 per cent and 76 per cent) is clearly in favour of films that present characters with extraordinary circumstances of some kind (be it war, famine, threat of assassination, etc.). However, these large clusters also hide deep differences within the two lists. As Table 1.13 shows, of the 76 per cent of films with an 'extraordinary' setting in the Elite audience list, the bias is very strongly towards the 'extraordinary' situation (84 per cent), whereas the Mass audience list shows a much greater balance among the extraordinary (30 per cent), fantastic/supernatural (48 per cent) and other/animation (22 per cent).

Table 1.13 Situation other than ordinary

Mass audience	Elite audience
Extraordinary: 30% (12/40)	Extraordinary: 84% (32/38)
Fantastic/Supernatural: 48% (19/40)	Fantastic/Supernatural: 16% (6/38)
Other (Animation): 22% (9/40)	Other (Animation): 0% (0/38)

Since our analysis shows both lists leaning towards the 'extraordinary', we thought it would be useful to look at how many of these films presented a 'life-and-death' scenario for their main character(s). Again, our analysis confirmed that extraordinary situations were frequently connected to life-and-death scenarios. There is a slight difference in percentages but Table 1.14 shows an unmistakable trend.

Table 1.14 Main character(s) in a life-and-death situation

Mass audience	Elite audience
Yes: 80% (40/50)	Yes: 70% (35/50)
No: 20% (10/50)	No: 30% (15/50)

We did a further analysis on this set of data to discover if the films had an 'epic' quality/ scope. The data suggest that the majority of films in both lists are indeed built around a notion of the epic: 70 per cent of films in the Mass audience list and 72 per cent of films in the Elite audience list can be categorized as 'epic' in quality. As Table 1.15 shows, there also appear to be a strong correlation between the epic and the 'life-and-death' scenario: of the films that fitted into the 'epic' category, most also figured in the 'life-and-death' scenario: 88 per cent and 75 per cent in the Mass audience list and Elite audience list respectively.

Table 1.15 Combination epic and life-and-death situation

Mass audience	Elite audience
Epic and life-and-death: 88% (31/35)	Epic and life-and-death: 75% (27/36)
Epic, no life-and-death: 12% (4/35)	Epic, no life-and-death: 25% (9/36)

Status of the main character(s)

We examined the financial/social status of the films' protagonist(s) in an effort to explore how class was represented. The data presented us with some interesting findings (see Table 1.16). Three results are particularly significant: (1) the remarkable presence of 40 per cent of films in the Mass audience list that have at the core of their narrative a main character whose financial and social status is not significant for the ultimate outcome of the narrative (the equivalent result in the Elite audience list, 24 per cent of the overall sample, is also significant); (2) the presence in exactly half of the Elite audience list of either a struggling or a poor character whose circumstances ultimately determine the outcome of the story; and (3) the remarkable balance in the Mass audience list, with effectively each status category scoring a third of the sample as compared to the Elite audience sample where there is a more marked difference between the wealthy/comfortable and insignificant to story groups (25 per cent) each and the struggling or poor (50 per cent).

Table 1.16 Relevance of status of main characters

Mass audience	Elite audience
Wealthy or Comfortable: 28% (14/50)	Wealthy or Comfortable: 26% (5/50)
Struggling or Poor: 32% (16/50)	Struggling or Poor: 50% (8/50)
Insignificant to story: 40% (20/50)	Insignificant to story: 24% (12/50)

In the Mass audience list there appears to be a strong correlation between films that have a happy ending with films where the protagonist's social status is not a factor in the narrative. The same isn't true of the Elite audience list where there is a much more balanced split between happy and unhappy endings, regardless of the status of the protagonist.

Location

Do the films reveal any particular preference for the action to be set in a particular location? We considered three groups: urban setting, non-urban setting, and unspecified setting.[14] Both lists show around 50 per cent of their films set in an urban environment (50 per cent in the Mass audience list and 56 per cent in the Elite audience list respectively), making this the preferred setting by far (see Table 1.17). However, while the Elite effectively shun films whose setting is not clearly defined (only 4 per cent of the sample falls under this group), Mass audiences shows a far greater preference for films set in an unspecified location since 26 per cent of films fall within this group.

Table 1.17 Location

Mass audience	Elite audience
Urban: 50% (25/50)	Urban 56% (28/50)
Non-urban: 24% (12/50)	Non-urban: 40% (20/50)
Unspecified: 26% (13/50)	Unspecified: 4% (2/50)

Race and gender

In 2000, California became the second mainland state where whites are a minority; Latinos have outnumbered whites in California by one million since 1998. Undoubtedly, nonwhites have reached an important critical mass through which their presence is beginning to be felt, even in the formerly white-dominated story worlds of Hollywood.[15]

The results in these two categories are relatively similar for both lists. In looking at race, we considered films in which a black character is central to the narrative (to the extent of being at the core of the actions that ultimately determine the outcome of the story).[16] In both lists, the black population appears to be remarkably under-represented, as Table 1.18 illustrates.[17]

Table 1.18 Black character who is central to the narrative

Mass audience	Elite audience
Yes: 6% (3/50)	Yes: 4% (2/50)
No: 94% (47/50)	No: 96% (48/50)

Women have a much stronger presence. Table 1.19 shows the presence of a female character who is central to the narrative (beyond simply providing a secondary love/sex interest) is 40 per cent and 26 per cent of films in the Mass audience list and Elite audience list respectively.

Table 1.19   Female character who is central to the narrative

Mass audience	Elite audience
Yes: 40% (20/50)	Yes: 26% (13/50)
No: 58% (29/50)	No: 74% (37/50)

Have these figures changed over time, given the impact of both the civil rights movement and feminism? Table 1.20 suggests some improvement. The results show an improvement post-1979 in numerical terms, but actually present a widening of the difference in percentage among films featuring a central female character and those without one (respectively, a −6 per cent difference pre-1970 and a 14 per cent difference post-1970), suggesting that the improvement might be less than at first sight. The Elite audience list scores a similar overall number of films, 18 out of 50 (36 per cent), but still confirms the under-representation of women in key roles.[18]

Table 1.20   Female character central to the narrative – pre- and post-1970 (Mass audience list)

Pre-1970	Post-1970
Yes: 18% (9/50)	Yes: 22% (11/50)
No: 24% (12/50)	No: 36% (18/50)

In terms of race, it should be noted that all three films figuring a black character who is central to the narrative belong to the post-1970 period, confirming intuitive notions of the rise to prominence of black actors in the aftermath of the civil rights movement, although of course this remains a very small figure (6 per cent of the overall sample) and still under-representing the number of black US citizens (13 per cent of the overall US population according to the 2000 census).

Presence of a well-known producer/director
Most of the critics and scholars who voted for the 'Best of' list explicitly mentioned the presence of a famous director as being one of the criteria for their choice of films. We wanted to see whether the Mass audience list showed similar tendencies. While there is a majority of films with a famous producer/director (again, mostly the director, much more rarely the producer), the split (58 per cent vs. 42 per cent) suggests that, for the Mass audience, while it may be preferable to have such a personality behind a film, this is not a sine qua non for success. Unsurprisingly, all of the films in the Elite audience list have a famous director behind them.[19]

Correlations

The when and the where
Some interesting results emerge from grouping two features of a film that have great importance, namely timeframe and location (the when and where). As we have indicated above, the Mass audience list and the Elite audience list have in common a (slight)

preference for films based in an urban setting. However, a closer look at this data reveals further interesting results.

As Table 1.21 shows, both the Mass audience and the Elite audience associate the concept of the urban with the present day. In the Mass audience list, 88 per cent of the films (14/16) that are set in present day have an urban setting. Similarly, in the Elite audience list, 71 per cent of films (17/24) set in present day have an urban setting.

Conversely, there is a much greater tendency to associate the past with non-urban settings: respectively 53 per cent (Mass audience) and 61 per cent (Elite audience) of films set in the past are set outside cities. In other words, the past is rural, the present is urban.

The other point of interest is that in the Mass audience list, films set either in the future or in an unspecified time are almost never set in the USA (14 out of 15 films): in short, audiences identify the future/unspecified time as belonging outside the US landscape, be it urban or rural (the respective figure for the Elite audience list isn't significant given the very small proportion of their films set either in the future or in an unspecified time but it is presented in Table 1.21 for the record).

Table 1.21   Combination of Timeframe & Setting

Mass audience	Elite audience
Present & Urban: 88% (14/16)	Present & Urban: 71% (17/24)
Past & non-urban: 53% (10/19)	Past & non-urban: 61% (14/23)
Future/Unspecified & non-urban: 93% (14/15)	Future/Unspecified & non-urban: 33% (1/3)

Narrative relationships

As Table 1.22 indicates, 60 per cent of films in the Mass audience list and 50 per cent in the Elite audience list show the following combination of features: out of the ordinary, epic, life and death situation. This a remarkably consistent result when compared to the second most common correlation (between out of the ordinary and life and death) scores only 16 per cent (Mass audience) and 8 per cent (Elite audience) respectively.

Table 1.22   Most popular combination of situation features

Mass audience	Elite audience
Out of the ordinary, Epic and Life & Death: 60% (30/50)	Out of the ordinary, Epic and Life & Death: 50% (25/50)
Out of the ordinary and Life & Death: 16% (8/50)	Out of the ordinary and Life & Death: 8% (4/50)

As we indicated in Table 1.14, most films in both lists adopt a 'life-and-death' scenario. We thought it would be illuminating to correlate this feature with endings. Among the films featuring a life-and-death scenario in the Mass audience list, two-thirds (67 per cent) end happily, with the remaining third (33 per cent) having an ending that is either straightforwardly unhappy, or ambiguous, or open.

Overall profiles

We finally looked at whether it was possible to identify a number of features that were common to a statistically significant section of the films in our sample. We did not expect to find 'the formula' but expected rather a recognizable profile of the kind of film most likely to be approved by the Mass audience and the kind of film most likely to be approved by Elite audiences.

Mass audience – profile

The features that generally characterize the films that Mass audiences have favoured over the years are: happy endings, colour, life-and-death situations, predominance of ethnic homogeneity, epic quality, and presence of a star. They all score 70 per cent or more of the sample. Given this, it's remarkable how *eclectic* the choices made by the Mass audience are. In particular, we were struck by the balance, often literally a 50/50 split, that the Mass audience list shows in terms of type of: audience orientation (adult vs. family), genre (with an even split among the three genre groups we looked at), source of story (adapted vs. original), presence of female characters, film setting (both in terms of time and location), and the presence of a well-known director. One outcome of our analysis intrigued us. Roughly, one-third of the sample does not fit into our overall characterization. This group may well represent 'another type' of audience. Whether it's even a coherent group is not clear but its size should be taken account of in any general description of the mass audience.

Elite audience – profile

The Elite group were always likely to provide us with a more coherent sample than the Mass group since it's composed of people who share a similar educational background and cultural awareness. It isn't therefore surprising that its profile emerges as a *narrow* one. A good example of this is that virtually all the critics/scholars participating in the 'great films' poll made it clear that they chose films according to one core criteria: the director. Critically acclaimed directors have, indeed, directed all films in the list. Several other features recur very regularly in the Elite audiences choices, providing a well-defined account of the 'critically acclaimed film' or cinema as *art rather than entertainment.*

The majority of films on the list (between 70 per cent and 90 per cent on average) have a famous director, are almost exclusively addressed to an adult audience, belong to 'serious' genres (the crime, drama, biography group), don't belong to the 'low' genres (the fantastic, supernatural and animation), are filmed in black and white, are unlikely to have a happy ending, and are never set in the future. The narrative, most likely involving a life and death scenario with epic undertones, is likely to be resolved with a clearly defined ending, probably unhappy. These films are also likely to feature a woman in a significant role but not a character from an ethnic minority. The majority of them (90 per cent) were released prior to 1970 and none after 1990, with the greatest concentration of films in the period between the 1940s and 1960s.

At first sight, this profiling appears to confirm common beliefs about the character of cinema entertainment. However, a closer examination suggests that it's a more complex phenomenon than is usually imagined. Where does our analysis support the established view and where does it deviate?

1   *Entertainment needs Stars.* Our analysis strongly confirms this common belief. Some 74 per cent of films in the list have a star present in the film. However, 26 per cent don't. A quarter is a significant enough proportion to indicate that Stars are not an absolutely necessary feature of entertainment. The contrast between the importance of Stars and that of well-known director/producers is obvious: only 42 per cent of the films have a well-known director/producer.

2   *Entertainment ends happily.* That happy endings are necessary for entertainment is another common belief that our analysis supports: 72 per cent of the films end happily. Again the same caveat as we made for Stars is necessary – 28 per cent isn't an insignificant figure. Unhappy, open, or ambiguous endings all have a presence in cinema entertainment.

3   *Entertainment is escapist.* If escapism is simply thought to be a preference for films with extraordinary situations (epic dimensions and/or life-and-death scenarios) over films with everyday life situations, then our analysis supports the belief. But escapism usually has a more critical edge than this view suggests. It's usually thought to be an evasion of substantial issues such as war, social conflict, unhappy personal relationships, etc. There's no reason, in principle, why films with extraordinary situations can't deal with such themes. Indeed, war films are a classic example of how they can. It would be necessary to make a different kind of analysis – a detailed thematic one – of the films to establish whether they, in fact, do.

Escapism is sometimes thought of as ordinary filmgoers' fascination with the lives of the wealthy. Our data about the status of main characters are relevant here. They do not demonstrate that such a fascination is particularly strong. Only 28 per cent of the films have wealthy/comfortable protagonists. A slightly higher percentage (32 per cent) has struggling/poor protagonists. And in 40 per cent of the films, the social status of the main characters is insignificant.

4   *Entertainment is light.* If this were true, we would anticipate a strong preference for the 'light-hearted' genres (comedy, romance and the musical). This is far from being the case. Audience preferences are distributed more or less equally across the three groups of genres. Significantly, the 'serious' group of genres (crime, drama, biography) is only a little less popular (40 per cent) than the light-hearted one (46 per cent). If entertainment is 'light', then we would also expect films oriented towards family audience to be in the majority. Our analysis does not support this. Overall, there has been a remarkable balance in popular films among those aimed primarily at adults and those aimed at families. Although family films have remained popular over the decades (46 per cent), they are outnumbered by films directly aimed at adults (54 per cent).

5   *Entertainment is socially conservative.* Entertainment is usually thought to operate in a sealed off area which makes it insensitive to social change. Its implicit social assumptions are thought to be conservative. Our results strongly support this in two of the three areas we investigated. Women remain somewhat under-repre-sented in relation to their overall presence in society (40 per cent of female roles central to the narrative as opposed to just over 50 per cent of the overall population), and it remains extremely difficult for African-Americans and other ethnic minorities to land a role as protagonist in movies that are popular with

Mass audiences (6 per cent of films in the Mass audience list).[20] The situation has changed over time but only marginally. The evidence in relation to the financial status of the protagonists is less clear-cut. If entertainment is conservative, we would expect wealthy characters to be dominant. They are not – there are slightly more films with poor/struggling protagonists (32 per cent to 28 per cent). The fact that in 40 per cent of the films financial status is irrelevant is harder to interpret. Does it indicate a lack of interest in and possibly uncritical attitude towards the way wealth is distributed in American society? Or does it mean that the films were concerned with other issues, which may be equally important? A more fine-grained analysis than we were able to carry out would be necessary to answer these questions.

6   *Entertainment is derivative.* A common assumption about film entertainment is that it's parasitic, that it depends heavily on source material from other media (novels, plays, comic books, video games). This assumption has been important for contemporary film scholars who frequently invoke the notion of 'packaging'. Our analysis provides very modest support for the assumption. Overall, 58 per cent of the films were adapted as against 42 per cent from original scripts. And from the middle 1970s on, the proportion has changed decisively in favour of original scripts (61 per cent as against 39 per cent).

The bigger picture

Data analysis does not reveal the 'truth' in an uncomplicated way. Like all data, our data could be interpreted in a number of ways, revealing a variety of conflicts and contradictions. The temptation might be to throw up one's hands and claim that it's all a matter of random numbers. William Goldman's much quoted motto 'nobody knows anything in Hollywood' is perhaps the most famous expressions of this position. It suggests that it is impossible to find meaningful information that is helpful for making films, whether they are regarded as entertainment or art. Many subscribers to this notion, especially scientists and economists, have adopted an even stronger stance than Goldman's, as this quotation from Leonard Mlodinow, a statistician and former studio executive, highlights:

> If Goldman is right and a future film's performance is unpredictable, then there is no way studio executives or producers, despite all their swagger, can have a better track record at choosing projects than an ape throwing darts at a dartboard ... But if picking films is like randomly tossing darts, why do some people hit the bull's-eye more often than others? For the same reason that in a group of apes tossing darts, some apes will do better than others. The answer has nothing to do with skill. Even random events occur in clusters and streaks.[21]

In essence, this view sees Hollywood films as randomly successful: no particular factor, such as stars, special effects, director's fame or marketing can make a substantial difference. Nor is any formula going to make any difference either. Indeed, for Mlodinow, running a studio is no more difficult a job than running the local dairy shop (*his example*). The view expressed by Mlodinow and Goldman is popular among film-makers and

Hollywood commentators/scholars. The industry is thought to be run by people long on egos and short on hindsight.

The work we have done convinces us that Goldman is mistaken. While it may well be nigh impossible to say what *will* work, it is certainly possible to suggest what *might* work with audiences. Surprisingly, the claims made by Mlodinow and Goldman ignore the difference between certainty and probability. If all they are suggesting is that nobody has the silver bullet, the magic potion, the exact formula for making entertainment, then we agree. Whatever the lessons one might learn about films and audiences, there remain enough unpredictable and unforeseeable factors as to make any attempt at slavishly following a formula both foolish and destined to fail in the medium to long term.[22]

Figure 2.1 Poster for *The Dark Knight*
(Warner Brothers/DC Comics/The Kobal Collection)

2   Sensual pleasure, audiences and *The Dark Knight*

> How is reading a sensory experience? In the experience of catching one's breath in surprise, the transfer of textual suspense into physical tightness in our muscles, emotional release in our tears, or when we shake our heads at cognitive disequilibrium brought on by an unexpected element in the composition, we know that our bodies and senses are part of the act of reading. Unconsciously or deliberately, we filter out distractions – background noise, temperature, the sniffles.[1]

As we were in the last stages of writing this book, the latest Batman release, *The Dark Knight*, opened worldwide to very large audiences and generally excellent reviews. The film has already surpassed the $400m mark in the US market alone (the outer edge limit for blockbusters these days: only a handful of films have ever done so) and could surpass *Star Wars* and become the second most successful film of all time behind *Titanic*.

The Dark Knight's success with audiences obviously makes it of great interest to us, especially as it has many of the characteristics that are believed to be audience turn-offs (bleak and violent tone, complicated plot, long running time). Our viewing of the film made us particularly aware of the importance of sensual pleasure in relation to audience engagement. We've touched on the issue in a few places already but the impact of the film was powerful enough to encourage us to develop our ideas, even though we only saw it when the book was more or less complete.

The place of sensual pleasure

In the thirteenth century, St Thomas Aquinas canonized views long held by philosophers and the church concerning the place of sensual pleasure in human life.[2] He argued that while humankind's search for pleasure is necessary, unless man is provided with higher pleasure, he will turn to lower ones. He identifies the former as intellectual pleasures (contemplation in particular) and the latter as sensual pleasures. If we wished to be polemic here we would suggest that in fact several centuries of art production and criticism have not moved the goalposts very far from St Thomas' position.[3]

Most noticeably, Kantian philosophy follows similar lines, albeit of course coming at the topic from a different perspective. In Kantian terms, pure aesthetic taste belongs to the act of contemplation. In this sense he would appear to reiterate notions of art for art's sake or art as 'purposiveness without a purpose'. When art seems to pursue a particular objective or result, this immediately reduces its effectiveness and positive effect on mankind. Kant is not against what he calls the agreeable arts, those aimed at providing sensory pleasure but he firmly identifies these as inferior to the 'fine arts', those squarely aimed at providing the higher pleasure of reflection and contemplation.[4] Some interpretations of Kant's thought have gone so far as to suggest that in fact 'Kant seems to deny that the feeling of pleasure can be the basis of any form of knowledge, even self-knowledge.'[5]

Of particular importance, we believe, is Kant's advocacy of a sense of 'critical' distance from the object of art.[6] Distance here was not simply intended, as Brecht and Pirandello would eventually employ in twentieth-century theatre, in a critical sense, but also in a physical sense. Kant presents a set of binary oppositions with distance and proximity. Abstraction and reflection are the activities that ought to take place in the space created by this distancing. These activities do have great value.

Within these discourses, sensual pleasure has little or no value. Indeed, fear of a possible collapse of the space of representation into one of identification has also been at the forefront of criticism of sensual (and popular) entertainment. In short, getting too closely involved means losing the possibility of critical engagement, the latter being preferable to the former.

More recently, members of the Frankfurt School reprised such concerns when formulating their views about mass culture, displaying substantial anxiety surrounding the very nature of mass-produced and consumed entertainment, one in which technology plays an ever greater role and the role of personal creativity is thus reduced. Inevitably, this view of sensual pleasure later became inextricably married to notions of popular entertainment, and cinema in particular.

In particular, writings on cinema in the early part of the twentieth century often revolve around fears of being debased by cinema's sensual pleasure and engagement.[7] In a more benign form that is in effect still with us today, views were expressed showing deep-seated concerns about the hypnotic nature of cinema, literally stupefying audiences away from their critical functions by providing them with cheap thrills and sensual gratification.

Given the strength of feelings concerning sensual pleasure in the centuries that preceded the arrival of cinema, it is hardly surprising that early film theorists should wish to distance the fledgling art form from sensual pleasure in an attempt to join the ranks of intellectual engagement as a means to validate their work. After all, cinema was already the site of a number of concerns and frictions: the dichotomy art vs. entertainment, the complex relationship between technology and art, the friction of having to conjugate the need for evidence of authorial intervention (the great artist) and the reality of film-making as a collaborative enterprise presented already enough difficulties to surmount. Indeed, film theory has spent the good part of the past century trying to prove that cinema is a serious art form and not simply another act in the life of the circus, a new technologically advanced fairground attraction.

As we have mentioned elsewhere in this book, film-makers often muddy the waters in this sense. Even when attempting to provide a positive view of cinema in relation to more established art forms, such as literature and theatre, these profound preconceptions about the division of sensual and intellectual pleasures come to the fore. In an interview carried out for the Writers Guild of America, of all places, Rebecca Miller – the daughter of Arthur Miller and married to Daniel Day-Lewis, herself a writer and director, in other words, hardly a novice – seems to make the case for sensual pleasure only to qualify it thus:

> By sensuality, I mean the visual nature of film and the pleasure the viewer takes in evocative images. Film gets into the brain through the back door, I think – the unconscious. In a way it is the non-verbal, primitive part of the brain the film-maker is courting, the emotional, child-like part.[8]

In other words, the pleasure that viewers take in sensual terms belongs to the unconscious, it is primitive in its address and child-like. These terms would seem to create the perfect negative to the positive of intellectual stimulation, direct address, adult pleasures, presumably confined to words and the verbal.

A direct, and perhaps inevitable consequence of all this has been the marginalization of the senses in the appreciation and understanding of how films work. Simply put, the critical system we have at present in film scholarship strongly favours an emphasis on intellectual stimulation over sensory engagement/address.

Given the nature of this book and what we have been arguing, we believe that there are some important questions to ask here. In particular, can we imagine a system where the critical distance between intellectual stimulation and sensory engagement is abandoned?

Since we are advocating the abandonment of the distinction between art and entertainment, at least in critical terms, we realize that this has consequences also on the debate concerning sensory engagement. One of the key ways in which art and entertainment have been kept apart is precisely by suggesting that one provides long-lasting intellectual stimulation (art), the other grants audiences more immediate, short-term sensory gratification (entertainment). We thus believe in developing a critical system where the distinction between sensory engagement and intellectual engagement is abandoned in critical and evaluative terms. We are not suggesting that the two are one and the same, rather, that they ought to be regarded as having, in principle at least, equal stature when considering the qualities of a film.

We believe that to suggest that a film is better than another simply because it makes you think rather than feel is thus wrong on two essential counts. First, it is a rather lazy way to assess movies and how they engage audiences at all levels. We simply do not know, after a century of film criticism, how films engage audiences at a sensual level, let alone how audiences respond to such a sensory address. Even rarer is any attempt at understanding how sensory address interacts with intellectual stimulation. Second, it is very difficult indeed to draw absolute boundaries between thinking and feeling, between senses and intellect, and the drawing of those boundaries is inevitably a political act, mostly in relation to considerations of popular culture and audiences.

Onwards, upwards... and downwards: *The Dark Knight*

As a large-scale, spectacular action film, the latest episode in a long-running franchise, with a hero who is a central figure in popular culture, *The Dark Knight* has many of the qualities that have proved immensely popular with audiences. Most people, asked to give an example of successful contemporary entertainment, would choose a film of this kind. But, as we've already suggested, the way *The Dark Knight* works might be expected to limit its popularity because: (1) its tone is unremittingly bleak, created out of sadistic violence,

Figure 2.2   Filming *The Dark Knight*
(Warner Brothers/DC Comics/The Kobal Collection)

Figure 2.3 *The Dark Knight*
(Warner Brothers/DC Comics/The Kobal Collection)

brutal interrogations, disregard of morality and common laws, death and destruction, subversion of the social order, and all-enveloping corruption; (2) the complications of the plot don't make the narrative easy to follow, especially as the pace of the film is unremittingly hectic and fast; (3) the ending is downbeat: Harvey Dent, the one idealistic character for much of the film, is physically disfigured and morally corrupted. The final scene sees him killed and Batman disappearing into an indeterminate future. There's little sense that order has been restored in Gotham; (4) the ostensible hero is unable to take decisive action to combat the chaos the Joker creates; even Batman resorts to sadistic violence in his efforts to overcome the Joker; (5) The potential heroine has abandoned Batman for Harvey and, in any case, is killed off in the middle of the film; (6) there isn't much humour. The Joker has the funniest lines which makes for black comedy at best; and (7) the film is long. At two and half hours, it's the longest of all the recent Batman films.

Our analysis of the most successful films did support many of the conventional assumptions about successful entertainment. However, audiences do show a degree of tolerance. It isn't, for example, an iron law that, to be successful, a film has to have a happy ending. After all, the most successful film of all time, *Titanic*, is the story of a human disaster. But, for the reasons we've outlined, *The Dark Knight* appears to test audience tolerance to its furthest limits. Its box office success indicates that audiences had no difficulty in coping. And at the screenings we've attended, audiences have been fully attentive for the complete running time of the film.

The image of *The Dark Knight*

Perhaps the single most striking feature in sensory terms for *The Dark Knight* is its size and physicality. This is not simply a film about big characters, big buildings and big explosions: its images and sounds combine to provide audiences with one of the most physically present films in recent memory.

Several strategies are used by the film-makers to achieve this. Each is designed to offer audiences distinct pleasures, both visual and aural. One of the most striking is the film's extraordinary array of vertiginous images and sounds. As the film unravels, audiences are made to feel constantly on the edge of a precipice, often literally. Canyons of steel, providing enormous heights into which one could horrifically fall or heroically choose to dive. From the opening few moments of the film, to the many shots atop huge skyscrapers audiences are not simply offered a bird's-eye view of the skyline of Gotham and Hong Kong. The camera peers down into the abyss below and for several moments in the film, the sheer drop provides an exhilarating feeling of danger:

> Watching the first dizzying, vertiginous overhead shot of the glittering skyscrapers and minuscule streets, I literally forgot to breathe for a second or two, and found myself teetering forward on my seat – timidly, I had chosen one high up at the very back of the auditorium – as if about to topple into the illusory void.[9]

The clarity of the images is another pleasure on offer here. The producer Christopher Nolan and cinematographer Wally Pfister decided early on to carry out tests with Imax cameras to see whether it might be possible to shoot some scenes in the large screen format for added impact.[10] As Pfister and Nolan recall, the positive results encouraged them to ask Warner Brothers to finance the extra money necessary to shoot part of the film in Imax:

> Chris spent some time figuring out what the post (production) path would be, and I came up with a realistic breakdown of the costs, which were roughly four times the cost of shooting only 35mm. Chris then set about convincing Warner Bros. to try something that had never been done before. I don't think that was easy, but among his many other skills, Chris is a very smart marketing person![11]

Nolan notes, 'I think the fact that it was unprecedented was a big selling point for the studio. They probably didn't truly get what we wanted to do until they saw the first test reel, which blew them away.' This 'unprecedented' choice (this the first film ever to employ Imax cameras for a traditional theatrical release) had consequences that translated down also to normal 35mm prints in terms of image resolution:

> Even in the 2.40:1 presentations [the 35mm ratio for the film], the Imax sequences (are) sharper and clearer, with improved contrast and no trace of grain … Many filmmakers are trying out digital cameras that actually capture less resolution and information, and we're going in the opposite direction, upping the ante by capturing images with unparalleled resolution and clarity.[12]

The choice of using 'real' shots, no CGI, was another strategy in the attempt to offer audiences a level of photographic quality and physical presence that has become uncommon, as Pfister points out:

> Here we are with our principal actor standing on the edge of one of the tallest buildings in the world. I think a lot of people will assume that's CGI … but when you see the shot, your eye instinctively detects something different, something thrilling and rare: photographic reality.[13]

Inevitably, these decisions on film stock and cameras impacted also on the choice of framing (Imax framing is very different from normal cameras) and hence the choice of what locations to use, how to design the production, and how to film it whole. The availability of the authorities of the city of Chicago to allow film-makers to shoot virtually anything they asked for was also paramount for the way in which the film addresses audiences.[14]

The issue of scale comes to the fore: huge film formats, gigantic skyscrapers, canyons of steel, streets that seem to never end are all designed to hit audiences: 'Chicago is the most spectacular-looking city, and to be able to shoot the smallest throwaway scene in such large-scale, real locations adds grandeur and texture'.[15] Of particular significance is Nolan, Pfister and Nathan Crawley's (the production designer) decision on how to design and film spaces, high rises in particular, given the challenges posed by having to integrate 35mm and Imax:

I talked extensively with Wally and Nathan Crowley about using the full height of the Imax screen, and when we scouted locations, we were very mindful of getting a lot of height and scale to really use that frame. One of the biggest challenges I put to Wally was that we would have a lot of night time photography where we put the camera on the ground to shoot people walking towards the camera, yet we'd still see the tops of the tallest buildings.[16]

These choices are then augmented by Crawley's design of the key spaces in the film. Most of them have floor-to-ceiling windows through which audiences are able to see high rises. The design of Bruce Wayne's bedroom with its marble floors reflecting like mirrors the great heights of the buildings around the apartment through tall wall-to-ceiling windows is in this sense exemplary of this strategy.

The size of the film is truly inescapable: whether on the ground or on top of the tallest skyscraper, this is a film that asks audiences to negotiate depth more than any other film in recent memory: where ordinarily audiences are offered images that work in terms of width, *The Dark Knight* invites them to explore depths and heights. This sense of vertiginous sensation is also emphasized by the action. There are countless instances in the film when characters are pushed out of windows, fall off the edge of buildings, or jump into huge voids. In other words, this is one of the key sensory modes of address in the film and it offers audiences a remarkable array of spectacular aerial shots. The size of buildings, the choice on how to shoot them, the realistic look of the shots, the depth of field all conspire to provide audiences with a sense of sheer size and grandeur that is indeed old-fashioned but extremely effective, as Emma Thomas, the film's producer, points out: 'It's like replicating that childhood experience of moviegoing'.[17]

A truck flipping on its head, a hospital being blown to pieces, a futuristic motorcycle weaving its way through a labyrinth of cars, people, doors, blasting its way through: the film never compromises in its approach to size: almost incredibly, all explosions in the film are real. In this sense, the film-makers choose to be truly old-fashioned and pull off one of the oldest tricks in the book of an entertainer, namely that of getting their audience to wonder: did they really do it? Are we seeing the seemingly impossible? In this, the film is close to magic: it leaves audiences gasping for an answer: how did they do it? In this sense, the film's appeal is in fact very close to fairground attraction and prestidigitation. This is not meant to be an accusation: cinema is as much a sensual experience as it is an intellectual one.

The sound of *The Dark Knight*

The sound of *The Dark Knight* magnifies the sense of scope and size of the film's images, though adopting a rather different approach. Whereas the emphasis on the former is to adopt a 'realistic' approach to film-making (i.e. capturing real images rather than creating them as CGI or visual special effects in post-production), the latter adopts a diametrically opposite strategy in that it goes for the hyper-real in both creating size and scope, and in helping the narrative develop.

In this sense, the approach to sound in *The Dark Knight* appears to be rather conventional for large-scale, spectacular films. However, while the approach may be conventional, the material used in it is far from being so.

In terms of sound design, Richard King and his team clearly spent a considerable amount of time working on the physicality of the design. In particular, the sound of body blows and fist hits are so loud, reaching so profound a frequency as to give the impression that they are about to break into a body, not merely hurt it.[18] This particularly visceral quality of the film's design is then stretched to its most extreme and uncomfortable levels in the interrogation scene. It is no use averting your eyes: the sound of Batman's aggression on a defenceless Joker is made inescapably present to audiences through the sound of violence.[19]

This is but one noticeable example of how the sound in the film invests audiences with hyper-real intensity and physical aggressiveness: the effect sought is one of visceral, oppressive engagement. Perhaps nowhere is this approach clearer than in the film's music score. Hans Zimmer and James Newton-Howard's music is almost unremittingly bleak and tragic in tone and movement, as one would expect given the overall tone of the film. However, even by the film's standards, Hans Zimmer's theme for The Joker, which permeates most of the film's score, is very unusual for films that hope to reach a large audience. The theme relies on one note, which has come to be referred to as 'the note', on which a remarkable array of distorted ascending tones, variations of volume (especially sound dynamics, with sound going from low to high volume within the space of a breath), and variations in frequency (employing the full frequency range, from the extremely high to the almost inaudible low) are built to form a disconcerting effect. This approach is not unusual for sound design (where film-makers have greater latitude in designing sound for effect) but very unusual for mainstream music, where traditionally melody and harmony reign supreme:

> The opening salvo, 'Why So Serious?' [The Joker's theme] is one of those tracks that creates a queasy and disturbing feeling in your bones, utilizing strings in a dissonant manner so as to throw you off balance, furthering the sense of disconnect and malice through shifting rhythms that violently jar themselves from the left to the right channels and then back again. When the track drifts into quasi silence, the only sound a barely audible recreation of a heart going through palpitations, the sheer terror is only magnified ... In a nutshell this may be the most daring and jarring music either composer has ever laid to tape.[20]

The aggressiveness of the piece is rather extraordinary in general terms, but particularly so for a Hollywood film that is supposedly attempting to reach large audiences. No catchy tune to whistle, no soothing harmony, no heroic theme: this is rough, aggressive in a very sensual manner, and unsettling to listen to:

> This is the soundtrack equivalent of a long, hard metallic drag of a bronzed violin string down a chalkboard- music concrete that becomes villainy at its foulest and most insane. Power guitar, strings, piano chords and god knows what all become the high-pitched squeal of fear before the Joker's knife slash. It's easily the most terrifying sound a soundtrack super villain's ever had, without real shape or melody.[21]

As well as providing audiences with a rather visceral soundtrack, the ability to capture on set dialogue in its full clarity provides the film with a rough texture that complements well the attempt to capture a sense of the real as it is defined by the film-makers (i.e. what you see and hear is what truly what went on).

This strategy in relation to voices and dialogue is made all the more evident by the fact that the film-makers were clearly prepared to incorporate in the soundtrack any 'accidents' that might happen on set. There is one startling example of this in the 'Joker crashes the party' section of the film. As The Joker surveys the room and the party guests, there is a distinct metallic clanging noise that happens in the background (possibly the result of someone dropping inadvertently something on the floor). This is rather startling, so much so that for an instance Heath Ledger seems to wonder whether something has happened (his head turns sharply towards the source of that sound in an apparently natural reaction to the sudden sound). Traditionally this is something for the cutting floor. But in a film where precedence is given to capturing the live performance of the actors, Heath Ledger, in particular, it is not removed but worked around.

This approach of using production dialogue tracks, rather than carrying out extensive ADR (Automated Dialogue Replacement, or dubbing) in post-production is significant in that it structures to a large extent the way in which sound is organized in the film. Virtually all the scenes in which The Joker appears revolve around his (Heath Ledger's) voice. Music is mostly absent or faded to the background and sound effects are kept to a minimum. The exception is usually a reprise of 'the note'. This is the case in all The Joker's key sequences, namely his address to the mob bosses, the Harvey Dent fundraiser party-crashing, the interrogation sequence, the visit to Harvey Dent's hospital bedside, and even the final confrontation with Batman. The only real exception is the big chase sequence where he tries to kill Harvey Dent believing him to be Batman. However, in this sequence, The Joker has very few lines, and when he speaks them, notably towards the end of the chase, the film returns to the previous strategy.

This gives Ledger's performance an added dimension as the soundtrack effectively singles it out and clears the air around it. This is important also in relation to a key aural component of Ledger's performance: his constant sucking, licking, lips smacking is perfectly captured on the film's soundtrack (it is truly extraordinary that little ADR went on, a testament to the quality of the live recordings). Ed Novick was the sound mixer in charge of production sound on the film, and the planning of the scenes where The Joker is in. Ledger's awareness of and use of his voice are a wonder to behold in their own right: he reportedly spent a month in a hotel room preparing for the part, and found voice training the most difficult thing. But there are clear signs of a very specific strategy, as Nolan remembers: 'I remember Heath calling up while I was working on the script and talking about ventriloquist's dummies, about having a voice that was high and low.'[22]

The Joker

As conceived by the writers, The Joker is the traditional disruptive figure whose *raison d'être* is the undermining of social order. What's distinctive about the character is the emphasis on him as an agent of chaos. Costume and make-up, the two elements that make the character immediately recognizable, are designed to make his disruptiveness more threatening and unsettling than in previous representations. The make-up is remarkable. Heath Ledger's face is covered with white pancake that is cracked and runny in places. His eyes are thickly rimmed in black, and a sloppy red grin is painted on, extending from his mouth to his cheeks, but not quite masking the terrible scars beneath. His hair is a more subtle, but still noticeable, shade of green. Make-up and hair designer, Peter Robb-King's remarks are illuminating about this approach.

> Clearly, there was a perception in the audience's mind of what The Joker would look like, but we wanted to get under the skin, so to speak, of what this character represents in this story. He is someone who has been damaged in every sense of the word, so it was important that we create a look that was not, forgive the pun, 'jokey'.[23]

It's this downplaying of the 'jokey' dimension that makes the character so threatening and unsettling.

Costume design supports this approach. The costume designer, Lindy Hemming, has described how she designed an ensemble that 'has a somewhat foppish attitude to it, with a little grunge thrown in'.[24] Staying with The Joker's traditional colour palette, she topped his outfit with a purple coat, worn over a green waistcoat. By combining foppishness and grunge and using garish colour combinations, Hemming imaginatively heightens the threatening and unsettling aspects of the character.

Heath Ledger's performance ensures that make-up and costume have maximum impact. We've already discussed it in relation to sound. Just as important are his movements and facial expressions. He generally moves fluidly like a dancer but his fluidity is often disturbed by unexpected changes of direction. His facial expressions are a subtle and rich mixture of sneers, threats, challenges and gleefulness. It is an extraordinary performance that deserves the high praise it has received. This combination of performance, sound, make-up, and costume is a perfect demonstration of how the varied sensual qualities of the cinema can be used to create an extraordinary character. The Joker is, without doubt, the creative heart of *The Dark Knight*.

We are not suggesting that the film is perfect, far from it. Indeed, there is not absolute agreement on its merits.[25] Hard cuts in the film (perhaps a result of having to cut from Imax footage to 35mm footage and thus having to reconcile two separate frame formats) often feel very harsh and threaten to disconnect audiences from the flow of the narrative. Dialogue for the secondary characters, Alfred (Michael Caine) and Lucius Fox (Morgan Freeman) in particular, seem often to belong to another film and consequently their characters are at best lightly sketched. There is no room to develop the only significant female character in the film. The direction of the action sequences, especially some of the chases, is so frantic as to become confusing (the geography of the narrative space is broken up to such an extent as to become unintelligible). However, to deny that *The Dark Knight* addresses our senses in an extraordinarily well-orchestrated way would be to disregard an essential component in the way in which audiences engage with movies. More attention is needed to the manner in which they engage, the level of this engagement and, perhaps most pressingly, how intellectual engagement and sensual address interact to form as powerful and seductive a form of address to audiences as that on display in *The Dark Knight*.

3 Alfred Hitchcock
The entertainer becomes an artist

I regard Hitchcock as one of the great artists of the twentieth century on a par
with Stravinsky or Kafka ... Hitchcock's preoccupation with the look or the gaze
... can perfectly well be seen in conjunction with Sartre's concerns.

(Peter Wollen)[1]

Figure 3.1   Alfred Hitchcock directs
(Universal/The Kobal Collection)

You know, many times people watch Alfred Hitchcock movies and they read
many things into them. I'm not of that school. I think Hitchcock himself never
intended anything significant. They are delightful but completely insignificant.

(Woody Allen)[2]

My goal is to amuse the public, not to depress them.

(Alfred Hitchcock)[3]

Although he died nearly thirty years ago, Alfred Hitchcock still has a strong presence in North American and European culture. His films are frequently shown on television and are occasionally revived in cinemas. DVDs of many of them are easily available, as are biographies, scripts and other material related to his work. There are numerous sites devoted to his work on the internet. His presence in minority culture, especially academia, is equally strong. His work features in the syllabuses of most university film degrees and complete courses with detailed examinations of individual films are often devoted to it. University libraries contain shelves of books about all aspects of his work. His films have also influenced fine art, acting as a stimulus for painters and video artists.

His reputation is a divided one. In mass culture he is best known as one of the supreme entertainers, a figure to be put alongside Cecil B. de Mille, Charlie Chaplin, Walt Disney and later film-makers like Steven Spielberg and George Lucas. He is most likely to be thought of in terms of the shocks and scares of *Psycho*, especially among younger people. Or he may be associated with the kind of Hollywood film-making that is defined by the pleasures of familiar genres, well-known stars, and high production values – films like *North by Northwest*, *Rear Window*, and *The Man Who Knew Too Much*. In minority culture he is generally considered to be an important artist, whose films dramatize profound themes through a sophisticated manipulation of film form. Comparisons are made with, among others, William Shakespeare, Franz Kafka, Oscar Wilde, Igor Stravinsky, and Henry James. For academics, *Vertigo*, *Rear Window* and *Psycho* are key films. *Vertigo* is the most highly valued: it is judged to be one of the greatest films ever made.

The split between Hitchcock's academic and popular reputations hadn't always existed. In the first part of his career, there had been general agreement that Hitchcock was an entertainer. The claim that he was something more was first made by critics associated with the magazine, *Cahiers du Cinéma*, as part of their project to establish cinema as art. Although it was initially derided, *Cahiers'* judgment that Hitchcock was not only an artist but a great one gradually won widespread agreement both within academia and in those areas where academia feeds into journalism and broadcasting. From his early days as a film-maker, his mastery over film form had been acknowledged but now, crucially, a thematic richness and depth were discovered in his films. Discussion has centred on the character of those themes – Catholic theology, psychological humanism, philosophy, psychoanalysis, and modernist self-consciousness have all been proposed as keys to his work. But whatever keys critics choose, Hitchcock's artistic status isn't questioned – even by feminist critics who have, rightly, been concerned about the treatment of women in his films.

The lively discussion and impressive scholarship that have given Hitchcock this status has, from our point of view, a crucial limitation – it has detached Hitchcock from the world of entertainment. Hitchcock regularly and unambiguously stressed his belief in film-making as a form of entertainment. And both in Britain and the United States he worked in film industries dedicated to providing mass entertainment. Yet in the books and articles devoted to the director, while there is often an (uneasy) acknowledgement of this commitment to cinema as a form of entertainment, there is no sustained examination of it. Since we don't share the generally low estimate of entertainment that leads to this neglect, we want to redress the balance and discuss Hitchcock as an entertainer. We begin our discussion by describing how deeply rooted he was in the world of entertainment.

Shakespeare, J.M. Barry and Dr Crippen

As might be expected of the child of a lower middle-class family in early twentieth-century London, Alfred Hitchcock's early cultural experiences were in forms of entertainment. His family's interests included most of the then popular forms, including theatre, fairs, circuses, and musical concerts. Theatre was the favourite form: the family made regular visits to local theatres. The entertainment they were exposed to was of a wide-ranging kind. In the theatre, for example, they saw drama that ranged from rough and tumble comedies to Shakespeare. The concerts they attended were mainly of classical music, including work by Roussel, Elgar and Wagner.

Hitchcock, as a child, developed an early interest in reading novels and stories. His tastes were similar to those of his family, rooted in popular entertainment and wide-ranging in character. At school, he was exposed to a conventional English literary syllabus, which involved the study of writers like Shakespeare, Daniel Defoe, Dante and Charles Dickens. Of these, the plays of Shakespeare and the novels of Dickens seem to have made a lasting impression on him. In his private reading, he had quite a range of favourite authors, including Arthur Conan Doyle, Wilkie Collins, John Galsworthy, E.T.A. Hoffman, Edgar Allan Poe, Robert Louis Stevenson, G.K. Chesterton and John Buchan. He was also a theatre enthusiast: in his teenage years, he started to frequent the West End theatres where he saw plays by John Galsworthy, Frederick Lonsdale and J. M. Barry among others. Barry's *Mary Rose* made a particularly strong impression on him. He was also a regular patron of the early cinema. After he left school, he developed one interest that wasn't rooted in popular entertainment. He attended art classes at Goldsmith's College and began visiting the London galleries and museums. His particular enthusiasm was for modern French painting.

Hitchcock's involvement in popular entertainment can't be separated from his involvement with popular culture generally. A fascination with crime, especially murders with a sexual dimension, was prominent in the popular culture of the period. Jack the Ripper, Dr Crippen, Edith Thomson, and the Brides in the Bath killer were all notorious figures. *The News of the World* established itself as a distinctive and widely read newspaper by highlighting criminals of this kind. Hitchcock developed a detailed knowledge of the famous cases, not only of the murderers, but also the lawyers and judges who were involved. It was to be an interest that was hugely influential on his film-making.

Hitchcock's attitude to women, which was crucial in delineating the heroines of many of his films, had similar roots. His well-known, primitive concept of female sexual attraction, which he explained to François Truffaut, is one of the stereotypes of English popular culture of the first half of the twentieth century: 'I think the most interesting women, sexually, are the English women ... Sex should not be advertised. An English girl, looking like a school teacher, is apt to get into a cab with you and, to your surprise, she'll probably pull a man's pants open.'[4]

Jonathan Rose provides a helpful perspective within which to place Hitchcock's cultural formation. Rose suggests that in the first half of the twentieth century, there were two competing intelligentsia:

One was middle-class, university-educated and modernist, supported largely by patronage and private incomes; the other was based in the working and clerking classes, mainly Board school graduates and the self-educated, more classical in their tastes, but fearlessly engaged in popular journalism and the literary market place. One appealed to an elite audience; the other wrote best-sellers and feature films.[5]

Rose names E. M. Forster, T. S. Eliot, Virginia Woolf, and Ezra Pound as representatives of the first intelligentsia, Arnold Bennett, Neville Cardus, Ethel Mannin, A. E. Coppard, V. S. Pritchett and Howard Spring as representatives of the second. At the time, the two groups were labelled as highbrows and middlebrows. 'Middlebrow' was (is) a term of disdain, suggesting a superficial, narrowly middle-class culture. But as Rose points out, 'It was also the direct descendant of Victorian self-improvement.' But Rose doesn't point out that, as well as having roots in the past, the middlebrow intelligentsia was also oriented towards the future. Because of its involvement with markets and audiences, it pointed to one of the crucial ways twentieth-century culture would develop. Hitchcock clearly belongs to this group.[6] Indeed, one of his early comments on his aims as a film-maker expresses the group's ambitions very well, 'My policy is to make pictures right here – popular pictures which anybody can understand. But without being highbrow, I believe in making them in such a way that they will appeal to the most intelligent people as well.'[7]

Except for painting, modernism didn't make an impact on Hitchcock. His interest wasn't caught by writers like Lawrence, Woolf, Eliot or Pound – the people Rose cites as representative of 'highbrow' culture. Indeed, Charles Bennett, the writer of some of his most successful British films, claimed that Hitchcock was the kind of person who would only read the 'dirty bits' in *Ulysses*. However, when he began to work in the cinema, Hitchcock was directly exposed to modernism and engaged creatively with it. During his apprentice days, he worked in Germany when Expressionism was having an important influence on film-making. And a little later on, mainly via the London Film Society, he came into contact with Soviet Constructivism. Both of these versions of modernism strongly influenced the way he made films.

Cinema as entertainment

Although the influence of Expressionism and Constructivism was strong on Hitchcock, it was also limited – he seems to have had little interest in the philosophies of the two movements. It's quite striking how he never refers to the politics that inspired the stylistic innovations of Sergei Eisenstein, Vsevolod Pudovkin, and Lev Kuleshov.[8] Hitchcock employed these innovations in the service of a rather different philosophy of cinema, *cinema as entertainment*.

What did cinema as entertainment mean for Hitchcock? His credo was a simple one common to most people who thought of themselves as entertainers. The starting point was the audience, which Hitchcock conceived as a mass, world-wide one. In his interviews he always makes the audience the centre of the film-making process. A film-maker's basic job was to meet its demands – Hitchcock didn't have any of the modernist antagonism towards audiences. People came to the cinema to be amused and not to be bored, he believed. His central aim was to have an emotional impact on audiences – on this, he agreed with Eisenstein. He also agreed with Eisenstein about the most effective way of doing this, through the creation and manipulation of images. But, unlike Eisenstein, he didn't want to go beyond the emotional impact. He distanced himself from film-making which had other aims:

> If there's one thing I'll never be able to do, it's turn my collar back to front and play the part of preacher. When people ask me what I think of movies that administer philosophic and moral lessons, I say, 'Don't you think it's up to the philosophers to teach philosophy and priests to teach morals?' People don't go to the movies to listen to sermons.[9]

His films entertained through the emotional effects that were created. He often used fairground rides as an example of what he was trying to achieve. Like fairground operators, he felt no need to go beyond the thrills and the excitement.

Manipulation of the audience was central to his idea of cinema as entertainment. It's a theme he returns to many times in his interviews and articles. In one of his most vivid expressions of the theme, he again uses an example taken from popular entertainment. During the making of *North by Northwest*, he said to Ernest Lehman, 'Ernie, do you realise what we're doing in this picture? The audience is like a giant organ that you and I are playing. At one moment we play *this* note on them and get *this* reaction, and then we play *that* chord and they react *that* way.'

It's the emotional effect on the audience that excites him. He went on to say, 'And someday we won't even have to make a movie – there'll be electrodes implanted in their brains and we'll just press different buttons and they'll go "ooooh" and "aaah" and we'll frighten them and make them laugh. Won't that be wonderful?'[10]

There were, unsurprisingly, contradictions and confusions in his view of entertainment. In the 1930s, he suggested that the demands of entertainment were oppressive, '[T]he power of universal appeal has been the most retarding force in the motion picture as art. In the efforts of the maker to appeal to everyone, they have come down to the simple story with the happy ending; the moment they become imaginative, then they are segregating the audience.'[11] Indeed, throughout the 1930s, he seemed to hesitate between a view of cinema as art or as entertainment. But these hesitations disappeared once he was working in Hollywood. He accepted the demands of the Hollywood industry, sometimes saying that it was important to make films simply to keep the industry functioning.

He was uncertain about the relationship between entertainment and realism. Generally, he thought realism was a threat to entertainment. As he famously said, he aimed to provide 'a slice of cake, not a slice of life'. He criticized Italian Neo-realism because he thought audiences wanted fantasy not reality. But he could be positive about realism: 'Now we have become more realistic and we can deepen our characters and give them another dimension,'[12] he said when discussing how the cinema had developed. A low-level realism was an important part of his working method – he took a great deal of trouble making sure that background details, like the design of character's apartments, were accurate.[13] And, of course, his work included some self-consciously realist projects like *Shadow of a Doubt* and *The Wrong Man*.

There was also a contradiction between how he claimed the emotional impact on an audience was created and his practice. As we've already suggested, he thought the impact was created by stylistic means, through the way images were handled. He claimed to have no interest in content – it didn't matter what secrets the spies were betraying (the famous McGuffin device). This was the one point that he came close to modernism. He seemed to be expressing an abstract concept of film, what he called 'pure film', a concept which was popular with avant-garde film-makers in the 1920s and 1930s. However, this commitment to abstraction doesn't square with the effort that was devoted to the creation of the script. An enormous amount of time and energy went into this. Writers who worked with him often describe the struggle to create effective narrative structures and engaging characters. And every critic who has written about Hitchcock's films has found it necessary to engage substantially with the characters and the narrative situations.

Towards the end of his career, Hitchcock's belief in film-making as entertainment was unsettled by two developments. The first was the celebration of his films by the *Cahiers* critics as major 'artistic' achievements, which encouraged him to have a more elevated view of his own status. The second was the emergence of 'art' cinema, as represented by the films of directors like Michelangelo Antonioni, Luis Buñuel, and Ingmar Bergman. Their films made him feel that his film-making was timid and conservative. But these developments came too late in his career for him to fully engage with them. Only the open ending of *The Birds* and the attempt at sexual explicitness in *Frenzy* clearly mark the effect of these developments on him.[14]

Materials and collaborators

Certain basic elements can be found in all of Hitchcock's films. They are crime, adventure, comedy, and romance/eroticism. It may seem banal to say this because, obviously, these aren't elements that are unique to Hitchcock. They feature strongly in the popular fiction and drama – novels, theatre, film, television – of the past one hundred and fifty years and probably longer. As most of Hitchcock's films are adaptations of popular novels and plays, it is hardly surprising that they have the same elements. Nor is it surprising that the dramatic devices employed in his films such as suspense, mistaken identity, picaresque narratives, characters as doubles, and glamorous settings are regularly to be found in popular fiction and drama.

Hitchcock's choices of novels and plays to adapt were remarkably consistent. They are the kind of choices that could have been predicted, given his cultural formation. Middlebrow would be a fair description of them. The general ambience of the novels and plays was middle-class, both in terms of characters and settings. Their authors wrote in a language in socially acceptable language of everyday middle-class speech. They didn't display the self-consciousness of the modernists or the social concerns of politically oriented writers. Their stories have an unpretentious quality; the authors didn't have ambitions much beyond telling a story that would engage readers. Their favoured method for doing this was the creation of intriguing narratives, most of which centre on crime, especially murder. Although they all attracted a decent number of readers in the first half of the twentieth century, most of the authors are now largely forgotten. Frances Beeding, Helen Simpson, David Dodge, Robert Hichens, and Selwyn Jepson aren't names that are remembered. A few, like Daphne du Maurier and John Buchan, remain well known and are still read. Hitchcock did adapt the work of some writers who can't be characterized as middlebrow, Joseph Conrad (*The Secret Agent*) and Sean O'Casey (*Juno and the Paycock*) being the most obvious of these. And Patrick Hamilton and Patricia Highsmith are exceptions of a different kind, interesting examples of writers on the edge of the serious/genre literature divide.

Hitchcock's choice of script writers was consistent with the character of his source materials. Most of them were writers, such as Charles Bennett, Elliott Stannard, Joan Harrison, John Patrick Hayes, Whitefield Cooke, and Samuel Taylor, who were skilled, experienced and unpretentious craftsmen and women. There are some interesting exceptions. Writers like Ben Hecht and Ernest Lehman, Evan Hunter and Raymond Chandler are on the same serious/genre divide as Patrick Hamilton and Patricia Highsmith. Hitchcock seems to have had a rather touching desire to work with more prestigious writers. At various times he tried unsuccessfully to interest Ernest Hemingway, Vladimir Nabokov and Graham Greene in working with him. He did have some successes, persuading Thornton Wilder to work on *Shadow of a Doubt*, John Steinbeck on *Lifeboat* and Brian Moore on *Torn Curtain*. (The collaborations with Steinbeck and Moore weren't particularly happy ones on either side.)

Hitchcock's preferred actors have more or less the same cultural character as his writers. Generally, he liked to work with established stars, as much because of the appeal they had for audiences as for their specific talents. The emblematic figures for his American period are, of course, among the men, Cary Grant and James Stewart and, among the women, Ingrid Bergman and Grace Kelly. Grant represents popular entertainment to the fullest extent, having begun his career in music hall as a song and dance man and occasional juggler, before becoming a Hollywood star, whose forte was comedy. Like Grant, Stewart established himself as a star through comedy. The main criterion for the choice of women was physical appeal – of a distinctive kind where beauty was combined with a certain refinement. Given that quality, he was willing to overlook other limitations.[15]

During his earlier British period, while the same kind of preferences are evident in the casting they aren't so strongly evident. He worked with stars such as Ivor Novello, Robert Donat, John Gielgud and Michael Redgrave. But with the exception of Novello, they were actors whose stardom was established in 'highbrow' theatre, in so far as this was represented at the time by Shakespeare's plays. So far as women were concerned, Madeleine Carroll was the first, strong indication of what was to become a defining feature of his casting.

In his American period, Hitchcock did work with actors from 'highbrow' art backgrounds. Hitchcock was no fan of the Method approach but he did use Method actors such as Montgomery Clift, Eva Marie Saint, Anthony Perkins and Paul Newman. The results were mixed. He had good relationships with Saint and Perkins and uncomfortable ones with Clift and Newman.

It was in the casting of secondary roles that the influence of popular entertainment is most apparent. His pairing of Basil Radford and Naunton Wayne in *The Lady Vanishes* is a classic example. Wayne had performed in various kinds of popular entertainment previously while Wayne had specialized in comic roles in the British theatre. Neither had performed together before but the inspired casting turned them into a regular comic duo.

Perhaps even more inspired was his casting of Marion Lorne as Bruno's mother in *Strangers on a Train*. Lorne had developed a speciality in comic eccentric roles when performing at the Whitehall Theatre in London. In *Strangers on a Train*, she was able to highlight not only the comic eccentric qualities of the character but also the character's grotesqueness.

Hitchcock's production and post-production collaborators (cinematographers, editors, production designers, sound designers, etc.) were almost all exclusively formed by their work as providers of British and Hollywood film entertainment. They were the kind of people who accepted the system's aims and were assiduous in developing the skills necessary for achieving those aims. Robert Burks, Hitchcock's long-time cinematographer, is their perfect representative. His early experience in the late 1930s and early 1940s was as a special effects cameraman, before he graduated to general cinematography in the second half of the 1940s. By the time he came to work for Hitchcock, he was well aware of the visual demands of creating popular film entertainment and had a range of skills to meet those demands. His skills are well described by David Badder:

> Burks was King Chameleon … in his skill in adopting the type of camerawork or visual styling which exactly suited each film … he produced, for a constantly on-form Hitchcock, a string of superbly lensed movies which ranged from the entirely convincing, impersonalized, documentary look of 'The Wrong Man', to the spectacular colorful location work of 'North by Northwest' and 'Vertigo', to the claustrophobic, single set restrictions of 'Rear Window'.[16]

Generally, Hitchcock's production and post-production collaborators weren't, outside of his films, high profile. They could be described in the same way as we described the writers, 'skilled, unpretentious craftsmen and women'. The obvious exception was the costume designer, Edith Head, since she was a regular Oscar winner and long-time head of the Paramount costume design department.

Two of Hitchcock's collaborators, Bernard Herrmann and Saul Bass, had significantly different backgrounds from the others. Herrmann, one of Hitchcock's most important collaborators, was formed first by the world of classical music and throughout his career he remained active within that world both as composer and conductor. His involvement with popular entertainment came by the distinctive route of Orson Welles' 1930s radio shows and Welles' early films. Herrmann gave Hitchcock's films a distinctive quality by displaying a modernist sensibility in his music, rather than a nineteenth-century symphonic one. Saul Bass, who had been influenced by Constructivism and the Bauhaus, also showed a modernist sensibility in his contributions to the design of titles.

Cinema as art?

Alfred Hitchcock was formed in a culture dominated by entertainment, worked in two film industries committed to entertainment, and developed his own philosophy of cinema as entertainment. How do these facts relate to his critical celebration as a major artist? Is there a contradiction between the biographical facts and the critical claims? Can they be reconciled?

In their introduction to a collection of essays published to celebrate the centenary of Hitchcock's birth, the editors, Richard Allen and S. Ishii Gonzalès, suggest that reconciliation isn't a problem.[17] They argue that the post-war revaluation of Hitchcock led to the terms of the debate being 'interrogated and reformulated'. The cinema was no longer perceived as 'mass entertainment' but as 'a serious art form'. But far from interrogating and reformulating the basic terms of the debate, their claim simply reproduces those terms. They contrast mass entertainment unfavourably with serious art. The traditional opposition is maintained: Hitchcock is moved from one side to the other.

Before a proper reconciliation can take place, a number of awkward issues need to be addressed. The most important are:

1. *Hitchcock doesn't fit the picture.* When asked about the themes critics had discovered in his films, Hitchcock initially didn't recognize their existence. The classic example of this is the interview André Bazin conducted with him in 1954. Bazin was a scrupulous interviewer and conducted his interrogation of Hitchcock with an intelligence and sensitivity that later interviewers have never matched. So his findings demand to be taken seriously.

Bazin asked Hitchcock, 'Several young French critics ... profess a nearly universal admiration for your work and discover, beyond the detective story, a constant and profound message. What do you think of that?' The director replied, 'I am interested not so much in the stories as in the means of telling them.'[18] He expanded on this response by giving a long account of the technical challenges he had faced in filming *Rear Window*. The only point where Bazin was able to shift the discussion back to the critics' claims was when he asked Hitchcock about the 'wrong man' theme. Bazin says that Hitchcock showed some recognition of the existence of this theme in his films. But the recognition was only momentary and he moved back to making criticisms of some of his films, mainly for their lack of humour.

Bazin conducted this interview when Hitchcock's films had just begun to be identified as major works of art. In later interviews, when the celebration of his work was more developed, Hitchcock's responses weren't so distant. But they tended to take the form of 'Truffaut has been looking at my work and he finds ...' However, he was still capable of responding to François Truffaut's claim that most of his work was 'strongly permeated by the concept of original sin, and of man's guilt' by saying 'How can you say a thing like that when in fact we always have the theme of the innocent man who is constantly in danger, although he isn't guilty?'[19] And when Truffaut attempts to defend his claim, Hitchcock says that he never let moral concerns get in the way of telling a good tale.

None of the attempts that have been made to explain this disjunction between critics' claims and Hitchcock's responses – Hitchcock was a liar, he was too modest – have been persuasive. They have mostly been made in passing as if the issue wasn't significant. But unless you take a strong anti-intentionalist position and believe that a film speaks for itself and that what its author thinks is unimportant, the disjunction is significant.[20] Hitchcock's responses, after all, are consistent with his cultural formation, the aims of film industries he worked in, the character of his associates and the kinds of novels and plays he used as sources for his films. Why not take them seriously?

2. *Art in the film industry.* The auteur theory has been central to the revision of Hitchcock's status from lightweight entertainer to serious artist. Since the early 1950s, there have

been many challenges to the theory and efforts to reformulate it. But its core commitment to art as a personal act, the work of an expressive individual hasn't changed. It has remained central to critical discussion of Hitchcock's work. The films he directed, over the course of a long career, are believed to show a consistency of themes and style. And this consistency isn't a superficial matter. It occurs at a deep level in the films. Profound themes, intricately organized, and articulated through sophisticated stylistic devices are evident in it. How this occurs in an industry, whose character changed radically during Hitchcock's career, where collective work with all its tensions and conflicts was the norm, and where substantial interference occurred regularly, hasn't been explained. Any theory of art in the cinema which is based on individual expression condemns the cinema to being a second-rate art because of the way it makes personal expression so difficult. Justification of Hitchcock's status as a major artist needs a different basis than this.

3. *The general audience and entertainment.* Do the qualities that critics think mark out his work as art – the sophisticated manipulation of form and thematic richness and depth – contribute to the enjoyment of the millions of regular filmgoers or are they features only appreciated by a specialized minority made up of academics and film enthusiasts? The problem is particularly acute because Hitchcock's achievement has been mainly established through close and detailed (often exceptionally so) analysis of their stylistic features. It seems unlikely that general audiences make analyses of this kind since they depend on a concentrated attention to detail and repeat viewings of films. And in many cases, the analysis needs to be supported by background knowledge of specialized fields like Catholic theology or psychoanalysis.

To explore some of these issues further, we'll look in detail at two of Hitchcock's best-known films, *North by Northwest* and *Vertigo*.

North by Northwest – creating entertainment

In his book, *The Hitchcock Romance*, Lesley Brill writes:

> To what does the romantic journey of *North by Northwest* lead? Generally speaking, critics of Hitchcock's films have answered 'entertainment' – 'mere' entertainment if they are hostile, and 'superior' entertainment if they are friendly … The romantic mode of *North by Northwest*, and of similar films, is crucial not for entertainment value but because it determines the sort of world and human nature the films represent, the moral ideas they embody, and the relation they imply between themselves and the rest of the universe.[21]

North by Northwest poses a substantial challenge for critics who want to establish Hitchcock as a serious artist. The film has all the conventional marks that are believed to indicate entertainment – an adventure/romance with a fast-paced narrative, light comic tone, and a happy ending. As a consequence, critics who have analysed it have looked for what they believe to be more substantial, 'non-entertainment' values. To give some obvious examples, for Raymond Bellour, the film is a psychoanalytic text; for Robin Wood, it's a social psychological critique of the modern world.

For critics like these, the entertainment qualities of *North by Northwest* can be taken

Figure 3.2 *North by Northwest*
(MGM/The Kobal Collection)

for granted. We want to challenge this taken-for-grantedness. We'll discuss *North by Northwest* as *entertainment* and not as a covert statement on larger themes, be they modern civilization, sexual identity, or Cold War politics. Our aims are to describe the kinds of pleasures the film offers audiences and analyse how they were created. We've tried to discuss the film in terms which are consistent with general audience response and not dependent on repeat viewings, close analysis or specialized knowledge.

Given our concerns, the most promising approach has been in terms of genre. A number of critics, like Lesley Brill, have identified the film as an example of the romance genre, relating it to folk tales and fairy stories. Analyses of this type easily lead on to questions of entertainment and audience appeal. However, as the quotation above indicates, when the analysis leads in that direction, a halt is quickly called. Brill moves rapidly away from entertainment, even if it's 'superior' entertainment, into different intellectual territory. For him, *North by Northwest* has moral/philosophical concerns. It offers a characterization of the world and human nature, the moral values that emerge, and the implied relationship between these and 'the rest of the universe'. This is a heavy burden to lay on a romantic comedy and it would be easy to have some philistine fun at Brill's expense. To do so would be unprofitable and unfair because much of Brill's discussion of the film is enlightening and we have drawn substantially on it for our discussion of the film.

Describing the genesis of the film, its screenwriter, Ernest Lehman recalled,

> And one day, I said, 'I want to do a Hitchcock picture to end all Hitchcock pictures.' And by that I meant a movie-movie – with glamour, wit, excitement, movement, big scenes, a large canvas, innocent bystander caught up in a great derring-do, in the *Hitchcock* manner.[22]

How did Lehman and Hitchcock successfully realize this ambition? First, it's important to note that when he said this, Ernest Lehman was referring to one type of film that had become associated with Hitchcock. A hero gets caught up in international espionage and, after a series of adventures, thwarts the enemy agents. The type is most purely represented by *The 39 Steps*. But as the title of the 1935 film indicates, fictions like this weren't Hitchcock's exclusive property. If anybody can lay a proprietorial claim, it was John Buchan, the author of the orginal novel. The popular success of Buchan's fiction encouraged many others, besides Hitchcock – Graham Greene, Eric Ambler, Ian Fleming and John Le Carré – to explore similar territory.

What kind of territory is it? As Lesley Brill suggests, narratives of this kind have their roots in folk tales and fairy stories. In them, heroes are brave and handsome, heroines, pure and beautiful, villains, wicked and ugly. The hero goes on a journey on which he has a variety of adventures that end when the villain is destroyed and the heroine is won. Clearly narratives with these features are adapted over time and take different forms. The relationship between John Buchan's fiction and the basic narrative is clear to see. Richard Hannay, his best-known hero, displays extraordinary powers in confronting his enemies before defeating them. But Buchan made an important adaptation. He gave his narrative a realistic dimension. He did this in two ways. First, he set his stories in the world of espionage, which, in the late nineteenth and early twentieth centuries was becoming a more important feature of international relations. Second, he wrote detailed and accurate descriptions of the physical settings of the novels. Buchan described his novels as 'shockers', which was an acknowledgement of his debt to the American dime novel. The most obvious feature of shockers is, of course, sudden acts of violence, especially murder.

Working in an established form of this kind, Lehman and Hitchcock faced two challenges. The first was that their version respects the basic conventions of the form and makes them work effectively. The second was that their version should be fresh and distinctive. In other words, the story should be the same, but different. Lehman and Hitchcock met the first challenge without any difficultly. The basic narrative structure is respected perfectly. The hero, Roger Thornhill, has a series of adventures that eventually lead to the villains being thwarted and Thornhill united with the heroine, Eve Kendall. The structure is a sophisticated one, which can be broken down into four acts and a coda. The attempts to kill Thornhill are used as punctuation points that mark the end of one act and the beginning of another. The opening act, which sets up the mystery, concludes with the attempt to murder Thornhill by drunken driving. The second act, which dramatizes Thornhill's efforts to investigate the mystery, concludes with his attempted murder in the famous crop dusting sequence. The third act, which shows the mystery beginning to resolve itself, concludes with Eve's fake murder of Thornhill. The final section, which dramatizes Roger's efforts to save Eve, concludes with Leonard's sadistic attempt to dispose of hero and heroine on Mount Rushmore. The coda concludes the story with Roger and Eve both safe and married.

Thornhill's adventures are both varied and thrilling. Interspersed between the attempts to murder him, he is misidentified as a spy and a killer, makes a journey across half of the country, is seduced and betrayed, joins the attempt to frustrate the villains, and eventually rescues the heroine. Lehman and Hitchcock display great inventiveness in their depiction of these adventures. There's hardly a sequence which doesn't display wit, imagination and a sense of the bizarre. The crop dusting sequence is the most celebrated but the villains' takeover of the Townsend house, the seduction on the train, the auction, and the fake killing are, in a variety of different emotional registers, equally vivid.

The form requires that the adventures are set in a fabulous land. In this case, Lehman and Hitchcock (supported by Robert Boyle, the production designer, and Robert Burks, the cinematographer), create a fabulous land out of a combination of distinctive marks of modern urban civilization and remarkable features of the natural landscape. Luxurious hotels in Manhattan and Chicago, Mount Rushmore, the United Nations building, Grand Central Station, the American flatlands (supposedly of Illinois but, in reality, California), the New York/Chicago supertrain, a Frank Lloyd Wright house, and the Black Hills National Forest make up an extraordinary tapestry. A clue to how the second challenge was met is provided by Lehman's remark that he wanted to 'do a Hitchcock picture to end all Hitchcock pictures'. He didn't want to make a film like *Foreign Correspondent, Saboteur* or the remake of *The Man Who Knew Too Much* that was a variation on the theme established in the 1930s by *The 39 Steps* and *The Man Who Knew Too Much*. He wanted to make one that was, in effect, a self-conscious tribute to these films, a film that would celebrate their attractions and avoid their weaknesses. To do this he had, first, to identify their strengths and, then, highlight them.

The ur-narrative Buchan created could be taken in different directions. Buchan took it towards realism, which is the direction Graham Greene and Eric Ambler also took their novels. But it was possible to take the narrative towards fantasy, which is the direction that Ian Fleming took. Lehman realized that, although there are elements of realism in his previous films, Hitchcock had a strong inclination towards artifice and fantasy. So Lehman highlighted these qualities in his script by inventing a narrative that is full of artifice. The central plot device – the story depends on a person who doesn't exist – defines the character of the film. The regular Hitchcock situation of the 'wrong man' is given an extra twist by the fact that there is no 'right man'. On the basis of this device, Lehman spins a story marked by improbable escapes, coincidences, disguises, and a miraculous happy ending.

Apart from fantasy and artifice, the other salient quality in Hitchcock's films is humour. Artifice lends itself to humour – it's hard not to be amused by improbable escapes and miraculous happy endings. And when the artifice is highlighted as much as it is in *North by Northwest*, the humour emerges freely out of the narrative. Because, for much of the film, most of the main characters don't have a proper understanding of what is happening, the story has some of the classic elements of farce. Characters are regularly at cross-purposes, interrogating each other in an effort to discover what is going on. These interrogations allow another kind of humour to be created. The dialogue is marked by a sarcastic wit, often generated by the idea of role playing:

VANDAMM: ...not what I expected, a little taller, a little more polished than the others.

THORNHILL: I'm so glad you're pleased, Mr Townsend.

VANDAMM: ...but I'm afraid just as obvious

THORNHILL: What the devil is this all about? Why was I brought here?

VANDAMM: Games? ... Must we?

THORNHILL: Not that I mind a slight case of abduction now and then, but I do have tickets to the theatre tonight and it was a show I was looking forward to and I get, well, kind of *unreasonable* about things like that.

VANDAMM: With such expert play-acting, you make this very room a theatre.[23]

Lehman's greatest achievement in his script was to make the hero a comic figure. Other Hitchcock heroes, the most obvious example being Johnny Jones in *Foreign Correspondent*, have a comic dimension but it isn't central to the character. It is with Roger Thornhill. As he famously describes himself when the Professor asks for his help, 'I'm an advertising man, not a red herring. I've got a job, a secretary, a mother, two ex-wives and several bartenders waiting for me and I don't intend to disappoint them all.' Lehman develops the comic potential of the character with a consistently inventive touch. Thornhill and his mother, for example, only have a few scenes together but the deft sketching of their relationship adds to the comic quality of his character and also creates a splendid comic character in 'Mother'.

Two closely related traits define Roger Thornhill's character: insouciance and wit. Both are key for the development of his eventual heroic status. Initially, he is hardly the stuff out of which heroes are made. If anything, he seems an anti-hero. But a clue to the sophisticated construction of the character is given almost immediately when he commandeers a taxi from a man by claiming that his secretary is a sick woman. The incident seems like a demonstration of his anti-heroic qualities but his quick-witted improvisation reveals an ability that will stand him in good stead in the threatening situations he'll find himself in – his escape from the auction room is a perfect example of this. The way Thornhill segues from charming rascal to romantic hero is very skilfully handled. Lehman keeps the character consistent. The skills that enable Thornhill to become a hero are consistent with the middle-aged advertising executive who is established at the beginning of the film. It is only at the very end of the film that Thornhill moves out of character when he becomes a conventional hero by showing an athletic ability hardly to be expected from a middle-aged habitué of hotel bars.

In fulfilling his ambition to make the ultimate Hitchcock film, Lehman was just as imaginative with his creation of the heroine. Eve Kendall is central to the plot in a way that none of the heroines in comparable Hitchcock films are. This is because of the ambiguous nature of the character who, for much of the drama, appears to be a villain rather than heroine. This ambiguity makes her more intriguing than the other adventure heroines who are, in comparison, clear-cut. Eve Kendall is, in fact, the most complicated of all the characters in *North by Northwest*. First established as a beautiful but mysterious train traveller, she is then identified as one of the spies. Her final and true identity turns out to be an undercover government agent. The ambiguity of Eve's character adds an extra frisson to her seduction of Roger Thornhill in the dining car. The seduction is perfectly conceived as Eve's witty and playful approach encourages Roger to respond in kind. The nature of her approach, however, suggests that the reasons she offers shouldn't be taken at face value. In the course of it, she reveals that she knows he's wanted for murder. The mystery deepens. Why is she protecting a man wanted for murder? Who is this woman?

The introduction of Eve significantly enriches the film's emotional texture. At first, her appearance maintains the comic tone: the sophisticated comedy of her dialogue exchanges with Thornhill is combined with the broader comedy of hiding him 'like a sardine' in the overhead locker in her compartment. Gradually her presence in the narrative introduces a new tone, romantic but with a strong erotic undertone. Indeed, there are scenes in the film like the beginning of the auction where the romantic tone threatens to take the film in a different direction towards the darker more intense tone of *Notorious*.

The script that Ernest Lehman wrote is a remarkable achievement. Traces of almost all the previous Hitchcock espionage thrillers can be found in it, especially *The 39 Steps*, *The Man Who Knew Too Much*, and *Foreign Correspondent*. What makes the script of *North by Northwest* so distinctive, 'the Hitchcock picture to end all Hitchcock pictures', is the craft and intelligence with which all of these have been combined. The way Hitchcock directs the film suggests he clearly recognized the power of the script and decided that his direction should support the script in an understated way. While the film undoubtedly benefits from the clarity and detail of the wide-screen, VistaVision format, little use is made of its other possibilities. Composition is usually functional: the main characters in a scene are placed centrally as if the film was being shot in the old academy format. Colour isn't an important dramatic feature – *Vertigo* is a striking contrast in this respect. The overall colour scheme is even and rather bland though it's occasionally enriched by the colour of Eva Marie Saint's costumes. It's only in the last sequence that light and shadow are used to dramatic effect. Apart from the acting and production design, the two

Figure 3.3 *Vertigo*
(Paramount/The Kobal Collection)

most important contributions are made by post-production methods. Bernard Herrmann's music and George Tomasini's editing contribute hugely to the fast overall rhythm of the film, generating both excitement and anticipation. The film does, of course, have a famous example of bravura direction, the crop dusting sequence, but this is untypical of its overall direction.

Audience response is the key test for the success of any entertainment. *North by Northwest* passed this test easily, attracting large audiences when it was first released. It also remains in the overall cinema repertory through its numerous, high-profile showings on television.

Vertigo – creating art?

> *Vertigo* can as well as any film be taken to represent the cinema's claims to be treated with the respect accorded to the longer established art forms.
>
> (Robin Wood)[24]

> [T]oday's audiences greet with a huge laugh Ferguson's reaction to Judy's protestations at having to wear the kinds of dresses Madeleine wore.
>
> (review of a showing of the restored version of *Vertigo* in 1996 in Houston[25])

Critics may disagree about the meaning of *Vertigo* but they have no doubt that it's a profound and sophisticated work. In critics' polls, *Vertigo* is consistently rated as one of the best films in the cinema's history, one of the films that most strongly justifies the cinema's claims to be an art form. Critics have described it as formally subtle, thematically complex, and stamped with the director's personality – all the attributes that, since the 1950s are supposed to identify a film as art rather than entertainment. Despite its reputation, when *Vertigo* was first shown, its box office returns were modest. Even today, there's anecdotal evidence that the film gets an uneasy response from general audiences, as the second quotation at the head of this section indicates. It's obviously very difficult to say why the audiences who saw the film in 1958 weren't particularly enthusiastic about it. The film wasn't previewed so there aren't even any audience questionnaires to help. Newspaper reviews from the time provide some clues. Based on these, reports of audience response at later screenings, and our own experiences of showing and discussing the film, we'll suggest a number of reasons why *Vertigo* produces an uneasy response from audiences.

Plot problems

One of the biggest challenges for authors of crime mystery stories is the invention of a plausible plot to sustain and then account for the mystery. *Vertigo*'s plot doesn't score highly on the plausibility scale. Hitchcock, himself, pointed to an obvious problem,

> One of the things that bothers me is a flaw in the story. The husband was planning to throw his wife down from the top of the tower. But how could he know that James Stewart wouldn't make it up those stairs? Because he became dizzy? How could he be sure of that!

This may seem a relatively minor flaw, although there are others like it (how come Scottie's vertigo doesn't prevent him from diving into San Francisco Bay when Madeleine plunges in?).

But there are more substantial threats to plausibility. The scheme for murdering Elster's wife is an elaborate one. The deception that is central to it depends on Judy Barton having remarkable skills to successfully impersonate Madeleine. She has to play a possessed woman, maintaining poise and assurance under the observation of a man whose training as a detective has, presumably, made him alert to deceptions. To do this she has, among other things, to have a control over her voice that allows her to change it from its natural, 'common' quality to a softer, more mellifluous middle-class one. If she has such skills, she's obviously wasted in an ordinary office job!

There's also a well-known structural problem about the plot of *Vertigo*. Why was it necessary to include Judy's confession? The information the confession contains isn't strictly necessary for the audience to understand the story. If it was necessary, why is it placed where it is? Isn't the game given away too early? The film-makers clearly realized there was a problem. When Samuel Taylor and Hitchcock were writing the final version of the script, there were fierce arguments about it among Hitchcock's entourage when the film was edited. The print that was first sent out for showing in cinemas didn't include the sequence. Second thoughts led to the print being recalled and the sequence restored.

Hitchcock said the reason for restoring the sequence was to introduce suspense in place of surprise. For him, surprise would have been created if the revelation of Judy's identity was held back to the end of the film. He preferred to create suspense. However, Hitchcock's explanation of the surprise effect only works on the assumption that the audience don't realize that Madeleine and Judy are the same person. Given that Kim Novak plays both parts, it's likely that most viewers will have some inkling that the two characters are, at the very least, closely related! Once they realize this, suspense rather than surprise is already on the agenda.

Whatever the explanation, the device used to dramatize Judy's confession, a flash-back to the tower and then the writing of a letter accompanied by voice-over, is clumsy both in conception and execution as Samuel Taylor, the writer responsible for the sequence, acknowledged. At a showing of the film some years later, he commented, 'We did it in a very inept way. That letter scene startled me. How bad it is!'[26] Despite the clumsiness of its execution, the placing of the revelation early in the second half of the film enriches the emotional texture of the rest of the film. It makes Judy a much more sympathetic character. Confessing your sins is one way of gaining anybody's sympathy. When it is joined with a declaration of love – she had genuinely fallen in love with Scottie while she was carrying out the deception – then the sympathetic appeal is even stronger. And pathos is added to the situation because the confession is only received by the audience, and not by Scottie, to whom it is addressed. A tragic romantic situation is created: Scottie desperately tries to recreate a dead woman, whom he has loved, while the actual woman is there in front of him and only too willing to love him.

The character of the hero

Middle-aged, John 'Scottie' Ferguson appears to have no close relationship with anybody apart from Midge. Other than the facts of his vertigo, little information is given about his past: he and Midge were engaged for a brief period, he knew Gavin Elster at college, he might have become chief of police. The character isn't drawn very sharply. It's not clear whether he's a long-term loner who has always been detached from the world or whether these characteristics are a consequence of his vertigo. Is he an oddball or is he an everyman figure, a victim of misfortune in the way anybody could be? Scottie is the central character, the prime focus for audience identification, so it's important that the identity of the character is strongly established. As it exists in the film, the character of John 'Scottie' Ferguson is certainly a difficult one for audiences to identify with.[27]

The problem undoubtedly derives from the novel where the hero is an even more isolated figure, although attempts are made to explain his isolation as a long-term problem – he was shy with women, he buried himself in his work.[28] When he came to work on the script, Samuel Taylor perceived there was a problem with such a hero and invented the character of Midge to give Scottie a more sociable dimension. In many ways, Midge is a great invention. The humour and energy of the character establishes an everyday, human quality which contrasts very effectively with the grand, mythic quality of the two main characters. The humour is particularly welcome in a film whose general tone is solemn and anguished. And Midge has a few scenes – when she sees Madeleine coming away from Scottie's apartment, her misplaced joke painting, and the scenes in the hospital with the mute Scottie, where pain and humour combine to great emotional effect. Barbara Bel Geddes's performance contributes a great deal to this effect. Very few actors could have got the emotional resonance she gets from this brief scene where she discusses Scottie's condition with the doctor:

> MIDGE: I can give you one thing: he was in love with her.
> DOCTOR: Ah? That complicates the problem.
> MIDGE: I'll give you another complication:
>   he still is.
> The Doctor studies her carefully.
> MIDGE: And you know something, Doctor? I don't think Mozart's going to
>   help at all.
> She attempts a bright, gay smile but it comes out wrong. She turns and walks
> away down the corridor.[29]

Everything Bel Geddes does in this scene is perfectly judged, especially the timing and intonation she employs in the delivery of her lines. Her performance adds great poignancy to what could have been a mundane scene. Walking down the corridor, Midge disappears from the film. Her departure is a real loss. The fate of a character whose emotional involvement with the hero has become increasingly intense and affecting is left hanging in mid-air.

However, while Midge enriches the story, the existence of the character also adds to the confusion surrounding Scottie's character. The audience is told that she broke off their brief engagement and yet she appears to be one who has the strongest emotional involvement in the relationship. Although he claims to be available, 'available Ferguson', he appears rather emotionally detached from Midge. Why? Scottie's detachment from Midge can't just be the result of his vertigo because their difficulties pre-date his accident. The question is the more insistent because the character is presented so effectively by writer, actor and director as an attractive, independent, intelligent, and funny woman.

Rhythm

Complaints are often made about the pace of *Vertigo*. Undoubtedly, the narrative rhythm of the film is slow, with sequences that seem repetitive and where seemingly nothing of great consequence happens. This was obviously a conscious decision, designed to dramatize the hypnotic way the hero is drawn into a situation that finally envelops him. Such a strategy was obviously a risk, likely to test the patience of audiences. To avoid this it was crucial that other elements in the film didn't unsettle the audience. But as we've suggested, some of the other elements do have an unsettling effect and the patience of viewers was inevitably tested.

Ending

The end of the film is both unhappy and badly dramatized, qualities that aren't likely to find favour with viewers. The last few minutes are particularly poorly dramatized. The pace is wrong, given the slow, cumulative rhythm that has been set up previously. In 45 seconds of screen time, a nun appears, Judy sees her, Scottie sees her, Judy falls, the nun tolls the bell, and Scottie steps out onto the parapet. It all happens too quickly to have real emotional force. The result is a too abrupt ending. The laughs that the nun's tolling of the bell sometimes provokes from audiences is one indication of the problem. It seems as if, by the time Hitchcock came to shoot this scene, he was tired/bored and wanted to finish it as quickly as possible. However, there is a more convincing explanation. In his account of the making of the film, Dan Auiler says that by the time they came to shoot the scene, the film was 19 days behind schedule and nearly a quarter of a million dollars over budget, which suggests that pressures of time and money resulted in only limited coverage of the action being shot.

We believe that the reasons we've just given make sense of audience reactions to the film. If this is so, then *Vertigo* is, indeed, flawed entertainment. In making this judgment, we aren't dismissing the film as a failure. We actually believe it has extraordinary qualities which, in some ways, make it a more significant film than *North by Northwest*. The way, especially in the first half of the film, the story is given a hypnotic, dreamlike quality by the combination of imagery, music and the rhythm of the editing superbly demonstrates the dramatic effects that can be created in the cinema. It's as if the film-makers had seized on the strengths of opera, theatre and painting and integrated them into the idioms of the cinema.

The end

As we've suggested, Alfred Hitchcock's work has been central to the campaign to elevate the cinema's status from entertainment to art. We think that our analyses of *North by Northwest* and *Vertigo* reveal some of the problems this has caused. We can highlight two of them.

First, because it's believed that personal expression marks out a film as art, *Hitchcock has been detached from his production context*. He has become the supreme auteur, the films he directed, the product of his genius. It's instructive to examine the indexes of books that contain critical discussions of *Vertigo* and *North by Northwest* and look for the names of people who worked on those films: Ernest Lehman, Robert Burks, George Tomasini, Herbert Coleman, Henry Bumstead, Robert Boyle and Edith Head. Only a few of these names are indexed and in the main body of the text, they are likely to be mentioned only in passing.

North by Northwest raises the issue in one of its strongest forms. Surely Ernest Lehman's contribution has to be fully acknowledged? Lehman himself in interviews and DVD commentaries has made a strong claim for, at least, recognition as the co-author of the film. Describing how he and Hitchcock interacted, he pointed to the complications of collaborative work. 'Hitchcock said to me, "Why do you keep telling me how to direct the film?" I said to him, "Why do you keep telling me how to write it?" To complicate matters even further, who is responsible for the famous crop dusting sequence?[30] It's usually taken as a supreme example of Hitchcock's film-making genius yet, with the exception of the non-use of some helicopter shots Lehman had included, the sequence was shot almost exactly as it was written. Certainly Lehman wrote it after discussions with Hitchcock but there's no evidence that he was simply acting as a secretary taking down what Hitchcock dictated. The sequence surely has to be regarded as a joint piece of work.

The most mysterious of Hitchcock's relationships, and the least discussed, are those with his cinematographer, Robert Burks and his editor, George Tomasini. Between 1951 and 1964 (when he died) Burks was responsible for the images on every one of Hitchcock's films except for *Psycho*. But what was the nature of his responsibility? Hitchcock was famous for saying that everything was worked out before he started to shoot. So did he tell Burks more or less exactly what to shoot? Did Burks add anything? The question is particularly pertinent to *Vertigo* given its visual richness – the flamboyant use of colour, the delicate manipulations of light, and the intricate compositions. Similarly from *Rear Window* to *Marnie*, with the exception of *The Trouble with Harry*, Tomasini edited all of Hitchcock's pictures. Was he no more than an editing assistant who followed Hitchcock's instructions? Again, the question is pertinent to *Vertigo*, given that editing rhythms are so important in the film.

Second, if it doesn't sever the relationship between Hitchcock and the general audience, the belief that the other distinctive marks of art are formal sophistication and complex themes, certainly attenuates it. The way *Vertigo* has been analysed provides a good example of the problem. The critic, Susan White, describes the range of the analyses of the film that have been made:

> A tale of male aggression and visual control; as a map of the female Oedipal trajectory; as a deconstruction of the male construction of femininity and of masculinity itself; as the stripping bare of directorial, Hollywood studio and colonial oppression; and as a place where textual meanings play out an infinite regress of self-reflexivity.[31]

Whatever one might think about the plausibility of any of these accounts, it seems unlikely a general audience would understand the film in any of these ways. Effectively they condemn *Vertigo* to being a coded document whose meanings are only accessible to a small group with particular background knowledge and the resources to make close, detailed examination of the film.

We believe that the campaign to change Hitchcock's reputation from supreme entertainer to consummate artist has ultimately been a retrograde one, principally because the basic terms, 'art' and 'entertainment' weren't interrogated. It was assumed that they provided solid ground to make the argument for Hitchcock on. But in the twentieth century, developments both within mass and avant-garde culture, made that ground more and more unstable. For us, the great interest of Hitchcock's work comes from the way he inhabited and survived on that unstable ground. He took on the challenges of entertainment: how do you make films that engage, amuse or unsettle millions of people who were divided by class, gender, ethnicity and nationality? What kind of stories should be told? What kinds of characters created? Do people prefer to laugh or cry? Do they want happy endings? And these questions have to be confronted in the context of a new developing mass medium with its paraphernalia of budgets, stars, technology, skilled crews, censorship, producers, studio bosses etc. In addition, a new medium like cinema inevitably had a loose, porous structure and was therefore open to influences from all kinds of directions: German Expressionism, Soviet Constructivism, Marxism, Fascism, Modernism, popular culture.

Hitchcock, like other film-makers of his generation, was in the middle of all this and had to find ways of handling the situation. His films are the evidence of how he did this. Reflecting on them, with all their strengths and weakness, takes us beyond individual achievement to larger questions about how the cinema has functioned in modern (and post-modern) societies.

One ambition of art is to get people to think what they did not already think, or what they thought without really understanding and the profound trouble with Spielberg as a film-maker is that he does not allow his audiences to think at all. He allows them only to feel.

(Louis Menaud)[1]

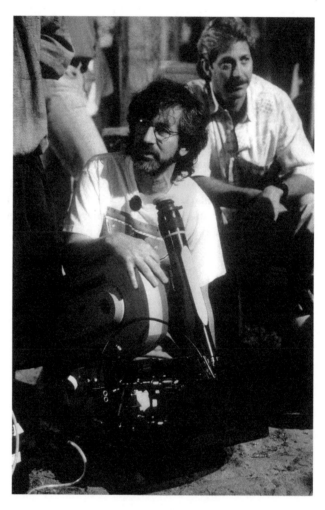

Figure 4.1 Steven Spielberg directs
(Columbia/Tri-Star/The Kobal Collection)

In one sense, Spielberg and Lucas didn't betray cinema at all: they plugged it back into the grid, returning the medium to its roots as a carnival sideshow, a magic act, one big special effect – the screams that greeted *Jaws* in the theatre floating back to the screams that first greeted *Empire State Express*, whose speed-freak instincts whip and blur into those of *Star Wars*.

(Tom Shone)[2]

4 Steven Spielberg, *Indiana Jones* and the Holocaust

> One thing I keep hearing about Spielberg is that he's always after money, making a buck. But he wasn't going out to reach their pocketbooks, he wanted to reach their hearts.
>
> (Gene Ward Smith, school friend of Steven Spielberg)[3]

> The thing that I'm just scared to death of is that someday I'm gonna wake up and bore somebody with a film.
>
> (Steven Spielberg)[4]

As one of the few film-makers whose name is recognizable to millions of filmgoers throughout the world, Steven Spielberg is Alfred Hitchcock's obvious successor. But, in most respects, Spielberg has gone far beyond Hitchcock. The range of Spielberg's activities and the size of his achievements are astonishing. He has directed 24 feature films. They extend across many of the established film genres: science fiction, war, comedy, political drama, and adventure stories. Their tone varies enormously from the sobriety of *Schindler's List* to the light-heartedness of the *Indiana Jones* series. The films have appealed to filmgoers of all ages – four of them are in the top 20 all-time list of box-office successes (*Jaws, ET, Raiders of the Lost Ark* and *Jurassic Park*). Spielberg has won two Oscars (for *Schindler's List* and *Saving Private Ryan*).

The success of Spielberg's films at the box office has had important consequences for the film industry as a whole. When Spielberg started work in the early 1970s, cinema as a form of mass entertainment was under serious threat. Cinema-going was no longer habitual, except for a limited core audience. It appeared highly likely that, by the end of the twentieth century, cinema would no longer be a medium of mass entertainment. Spielberg made a major contribution to stopping this from happening.

All of this would be a substantial achievement on its own, but Spielberg has also:

- produced a substantial number of films (including *Flags of Our Fathers, Back to the Future* and *Poltergeist*);
- done substantial work in television, producing successful series like *ER* and *Band of Brothers*;
- created his own production company, Amblin' Films, and was part of the trio who created the new Hollywood studio, DreamWorks;
- been socially and politically active: establishing the Shoah Visual History Foundation (a world-wide programme to record the testimonies of Holocaust survivors) and vigorously supporting the Democratic Party, especially when Bill Clinton was President.

For all his achievements, there's one area where Spielberg hasn't outdone Hitchcock. He isn't celebrated as one of the cinema's major artists. No adulatory critics, like François Truffaut, Robin Wood or Eric Rohmer and Claude Chabrol, have emerged to champion his work. On the face of it, the reason for this is obvious, Spielberg's close association with entertainment. He stands out from his contemporaries (with the exception of George Lucas) for the way he explicitly and consistently identifies himself as a mass entertainer:

> I've always had an urge to please the audience, to please people other than myself. I never thought about compromising my own self-respect. I was into putting on a great show and sitting back and enjoying the audience participation. I felt more like P.T. Barnum than John Ford for a lot of my career. And I wasn't ashamed of that. I've always thought that filling every seat in every theatre in America was the ultimate vindication and validation.[5]

But this reason isn't as convincing as it first appears. After all, Hitchcock also identified himself as a mass entertainer and this didn't prevent him from being acclaimed as a major film-maker. Why haven't critics celebrated Spielberg's work?

1. Spielberg's films are dismissed not simply because they are entertainments but also because they display the features of entertainment that are thought to make it limited and trivial – spectacle, happy endings, sentimentality, cute characters (especially aliens and children), naïveté. Spielberg is accused of creating a 'un-ironic' cinema, which certainly isn't something Hitchcock could be accused of.

2. The political situation in the 1970s, when Spielberg established himself as a film-maker was, was very different from the political situation in the late 1940s/early 1950s, when *Cahiers du Cinéma* started to celebrate Hitchcock's work. The *Cahiers* critics were writing just after the Second World War had ended. America was regarded benignly because of its contribution to the defeat of Fascism. But by the 1970s, political attitudes to America had radically changed, principally because of the Vietnam War. Widespread opposition to the war developed into a much more general opposition to America's international role, its economic domination, and the pervasiveness of its ideology and culture. Hollywood was inevitably drawn into the political debate. It was identified as a major instrument of ideological domination – Jean Luc-Godard's simplistic and crude tirades against Hollywood usually made Spielberg the villain of the piece. Because of Hollywood's commitment to entertainment, a kind of shorthand equation was established:

Hollywood = entertainment = bourgeois ideological domination

In such a context, the work of a director like Spielberg, who identified himself as an entertainer, was hardly likely to be celebrated.

3. Spielberg (together with George Lucas) became a villain in a narrative about the decline of Hollywood in the 1970s, a story of how entertainment supplanted art. Peter Biskind told this story most persuasively in his widely read account of Hollywood in the 1970s, *Easy Riders, Raging Bulls*:

Lucas and Spielberg returned the '70s audience, grown sophisticated on a diet of European and New Hollywood films, to the simplicities of the pre-'60s Golden Age of movies ... They marched backwards through the looking glass, producing pictures that were the mirror opposites of the New Hollywood films of their peers. They were, as Kael first pointed out, infantilizing the audience, reconstituting the spectator as child, then overwhelming him and her with sound and spectacle, obliterating irony, aesthetic self-consciousness, and critical reflection.[6]

Clearly, Spielberg's work acts as a lightning conductor for anxieties about entertainment. It attracts all the familiar objections: entertainment is cheap and trivial, and/or it's disguised ideology, and/or it's a childish mode. These objections aren't specific to Spielberg's work: they are based on general, widely held views. Spielberg stands out because he doesn't share these views and has consistently expressed positive attitudes to entertainment. He also stands out because of the enormous success he's had in creating it!

Growing up with mass entertainment

Spielberg's cultural formation was squarely within mass entertainment. Born in 1946, he grew up at a time when it had become pervasive. His involvement was typical for boys growing up outside major urban complexes. Film and television were central. His initial exposure was to the kind of entertainment that attracts adjectives such as 'light' and 'escapist'. He saw films and television programmes that mainly reflected his parents' tastes. Spielberg says the films were of a 'general audience' kind: *The Court Jester* with Danny Kaye, *Funny Face* with Audrey Hepburn, and Disney cartoons and adventure stories. His television viewing was similar: programmes with well-known performers like Sid Caesar and Imogene Coca as well as long-running series like *The Honeymooners*.

However, as he grew older, he saw a wider variety of films, from cartoons and Tarzan films to more ambitious efforts, like *Moby Dick* and *The Searchers*. He was exposed to other sources of mass entertainment, the most significant which was science fiction. Taking advantage of the magazines and paperbacks, his father, a fan, left around the house, Spielberg developed an extensive knowledge of sci-fi literature. He also read comics, becoming a fan of the superhero genre (Batman and Superman). And he discovered *Mad* magazine and Lenny Bruce records. By his middle teens, Spielberg had had a full exposure to the most popular forms of mass entertainment.

Crucially, he also started to make films, the first when he was only 8 years old. By the time he was 18, he was an experienced film-maker, having made about 20 films of a varied kind: home movies, documentaries, westerns, film noir, and adventure films. He had almost total responsibility for their creation, acting as producer, director, scriptwriter, cinematographer, sound man, and editor. They were shown to a variety of audiences and received more public exposure than is usual for amateur film-makers – there aren't too many 17-year-olds who have had a full-scale premiere at the local cinema for their two-hour epic.

Of all his youthful enthusiasms, film-making engaged his imagination in the most powerful way. He learned the complete range of craft skills. Even more significantly, he became aware of the satisfaction to be had from audience response. He's spoken on several occasions about the kick he got from the way audiences responded to his early efforts. He recalled that, when he showed a film to an audience of his fellow boy scouts, they 'cheered and applauded and laughed at what I did, and I really wanted to do that, to please again'.[7]

Was there anything in his formation that would have distanced him from mass entertainment or encouraged him to take a critical attitude towards it? High culture, in the form of classical music had a strong presence in his home life – his mother, who had hoped to become a concert pianist, regularly played the piano and listened to records. But there's no evidence that classical music was presented as significantly different from mass entertainment, or as a possible challenge to it. And Spielberg never developed an interest in other forms of high culture that might have distanced him from mass entertainment. Gene Ward Smith, a close friend in their teenage years, has provided an illuminating description of his tastes at that time. He told Joseph McBride,

> Spielberg was peculiar in that he was both well read and *not* well read ... Inside the sci-fi, fantasy-adventure field he was well read but outside that field he wasn't. I would try to get him to read all these books – I would talk about Ralph Ellison's *Invisible Man*, which came up during a discussion of H.G. Wells. I also talked about James Baldwin's essays, *The Fire Next Time*, and probably *Nobody Knows My Name*, and *Notes of a Native Son* ... I certainly would not have mentioned *Giovanni's Room*, despite my particular liking for that book. When I brought up something like *The Brothers Karamazov*, he would respond like he knew what I was talking about, but we would move on to something else; he would burble on about sci-fi books. I kept trying and it was hopeless. I tried to get him to read Joyce, for instance, pushing *Ulysses* as a kind of book which was fantastic without being fantasy and carefully avoiding any suggestion that it might be difficult reading, but I couldn't sell him on it.[8]

Overall, there was little in Spielberg's cultural formation up to the age of 18 that challenged his involvement with mass entertainment. But some of his tastes – *Mad* magazine and Lenny Bruce – took him towards its boundaries, to areas where mass entertainment made contact with the counter-culture. His liking for Bruce was particularly significant because it marked the first signs of a social conscience. A friend who shared his enthusiasm for Bruce says it began from their joint commitment to the civil rights movement. As a Jew, Spielberg responded to the way Bruce linked Jews with Blacks, 'Negroes are all Jews.' This nascent social conscience didn't fully emerge until later in Spielberg's life. When it did, it had a significant effect on his film-making.

Modernizing entertainment

The first serious challenge to Spielberg's ideas came when he took the first steps towards becoming a professional film director. At the same time as he was hanging out at Universal Studios, observing established professionals at work, he encountered a different kind of cinema – the cinema of *The Seventh Seal*, *L'Avventura*, *La Dolce Vita*, *Breathless*, *The 400 Blows*. The work of directors such as Ingmar Bergman, Michelangelo Antonioni,

Jean-Luc Godard, and François Truffaut was a revelation to him. He appeared to be committed to art rather than entertainment. His first films show the impact of these new films on him. *Duel* had the qualities that Godard and Truffaut admired in the Hollywood B-picture: vividness, intensity and simplicity. *The Sugarland Express*, with its loose narrative structure, unheroic central characters, and shifting dramatic tone, echoes the New Wave films (or the New Wave films mediated through *Bonnie and Clyde*). Spielberg recalled that, at the time he was offered *Jaws*, 'I didn't know who I was. I wanted to make a movie that left its mark, not at the box office, but on people's consciousness. I wanted to be Antonioni, Bob Rafelson ... Who wants to be known as a shark and truck director?'[9] *Jaws* proved to be a turning point for Spielberg. His ambition to be Antonioni was sidelined, although it was to resurface later in his career. The film's success meant that he did become best known as a shark and truck director, or, more exactly, as a shark, extraterrestrial and dinosaur director. It also established him as a major contributor to the success of Hollywood's new strategy for maintaining itself as a provider of mass entertainment

This centrepiece of this strategy was the creation of 'big' films, first called 'Roadshow' films and then 'Blockbusters'. They were, in essence, spectacular films that were heavily publicized. The early films of this type tended to be ponderous and culturally traditional, drawing on well-known historical or biblical stories (*Ben Hur*, *Spartacus*, *How the West Was Won*) or being adaptations of successful stage musicals (*South Pacific*, *West Side Story*, *My Fair Lady*). They were also stylistically conservative, they tended to cost a great deal to make.

Spielberg, joined swiftly by George Lucas, became the spearhead for film-making with a more modern character. It was shaped by a different kind of consciousness: a consciousness formed by sci-fi literature, *Mad* magazine, adventure serials and cartoon films. It was stylistically radical, influenced, on the one hand, by the freedom the New Wave films displayed and, on the other, by technical innovations which among other things, revolutionized the character of both sound and visual effects. Spielberg and Lucas also demonstrated that it was possible to make spectacular films relatively cheaply.

This approach received crucial support from innovations in both the distribution and exhibition sectors. The old fixed patterns of releasing films were abandoned. Films received simultaneous widespread releases and were shown in cinemas for as long as audiences held up. Cinemas were redesigned. The new 'multiplexes' were superior in most respects to the old, individual cinemas they replaced. Usually part of leisure/entertainment complexes with convenient shops and restaurants, they had better parking facilities and were more easily accessible. The viewing experience was much enhanced: more comfortable seats, better sight lines, and vastly improved sound reproduction. By the 1980s, Spielberg was established as a major figure in the new, more modern version of cinema as mass entertainment that these developments had created.

Audiences, images and sounds

Spielberg makes a first connection with his audiences through the use of familiar genres. He respects the basic genre conventions, offering audiences the kind of pleasures they expect. The films are made distinctive by the way their emotional impact is heightened.

This effect isn't peculiar to Spielberg. From the late 1960s on, one of the ways film-makers tried to create a more modern cinema was to make films with a stronger emotional impact, films whose effect was intense and visceral, like that of a rock concert. One consequence was a concentration on violence and sexuality, which inevitably produced films aimed at adult audiences. Film-makers taking this approach tended to think of themselves as artists and justify their approach with familiar artistic claims of extending the boundaries or breaking taboos. Spielberg, however, has rarely lost sight of the family audience. There certainly is violence in his films but it's generally not between humans but between humans and animals, like sharks and dinosaurs. When he's handled these situations, he's never been hesitant about heightening the emotional impact. But, given the audience he aims at, he tends to focus on less threatening emotions. Mystery, wonder, and curiosity are feelings that are regularly dramatized in his films, which is why science fiction is a favoured genre.

Technological innovations, especially in areas like sound and visual effects, have enormously helped Spielberg. One of his great strengths as a director has been his ability to appreciate the dramatic potential of these developments – indeed, to help their development along as he did with computer-generated image creation for *Jurassic Park*. As the distinguished palaeontologist, Stephen Jay Gould, argues, in his review of *Jurassic Park*, effects created in this way deserve more respect than they usually get:

> The dinosaur scenes are spectacular. Intellectuals too often either pay no attention to such technical wizardry or, even worse, actually disdain special effects with such dismissive epithets as 'merely mechanical'. I find such small-minded parochialism outrageous. Nothing can be more complex than a living organism, with all the fractal geometry of its form and behaviour ... The use of technology to render accurate and believable animals therefore becomes one of the greatest all-time challenges to human ingenuity ... Yes, *Jurassic Park* is 'just' a movie – but for this very reason, it had freedom and money to develop techniques of reconstruction, particularly computer generation or CG, to new heights of astonishing realism.[10]

Spielberg sets out to engage audiences at all levels of a film, paying as much attention to images, sounds and rhythms as he does to story, characters and settings. One of his great talents is the ability to manipulate sounds and images to maximum effect. His basic film aesthetic is virtually a silent cinema one. Images supported by music are a key way that he engages audiences. Well-defined points of visual interest always ensure that the audience has something interesting to look at. Lighting is a great instrument for doing this: it usually makes a large contribution to the character of an image. He and his cinematographers regularly go for bold effects, using the sun or the moon as light sources. Back lighting is a much favoured strategy. The perfect illustration of this is an image in *Empire of the Sun* when a very early morning sun backlights the figures of the Japanese airmen as they make a ceremonial departure on a suicide mission. He's also capable of getting his cinematographers to produce more subtle effects. In an early scene in the film, gentle daylight gleams on the highly polished surfaces of large, black cars, indicating the bourgeois comfort of Europeans' life in China.

Lighting isn't the only way that images are given interest. Camera movement and composition are almost as important. Spielberg is particularly good at working with his cinematographers to make dynamic use of wide-screen space, knowing when it's dramatically necessary to fill space and when it's best left empty. The images receive strong support from music, which is used consistently throughout the film to heighten the dramatic effect of the images on the audience. The use of music in this way is, of course, a long-established convention, prone to cliché. Spielberg has been fortunate that his long-time collaborator, John Williams, is both a prolific and an inventive composer. He has also been fortunate to work with sound designers of a similar quality, like Ben Burtt and Gary Rydstrom, who have provided him with such memorable effects as E.T.'s voice and the dinosaur sounds in *Jurassic Park*. In the latter film, the roars of the dinosaurs do as much to create a sense of awe and terror as the visual effects that Stephen Jay Gould praises.

Spielberg's approach to entertaining audiences has obviously been enormously successful. Are there any groups who've remained immune to its appeal? Detailed breakdowns of the composition of audiences for Spielberg's films either don't exist or aren't easily available. The existing data confirm what personal observation and anecdotal evidence suggest: their appeal reaches well beyond the core cinema audience of young, unmarried people in the 15–30 year age group. Crucially, they have a strong appeal for people who are at best occasional filmgoers (from younger and older age groups, families). There's no strong evidence that the films don't appeal to any groups, though questions have been raised about the response of black audiences in the United States. In his book about American audiences, Tom Stempel reports that a group of black students from Oakland who went to see *Schindler's List* 'talked and laughed during the scenes of the horrors of The Holocaust and eventually had to be removed from the theatre'.[11] A black journalist argued that their reaction was caused by a general disenchantment with Hollywood cinema because of the way blacks are represented. Another explanation is that they simply weren't prepared for the kind of film they were going to see. Support for this explanation is provided by the fact that a similar incident occurred in Los Angeles but this time the unsympathetic audience was white teenagers who, again, weren't made aware of the kind of film they were going to see.

What evidence there is about audience response to *The Color Purple* also suggests that the responses of black audiences are not particularly different from those of white or any other ethnic groups. Of all the films Spielberg has directed, *The Color Purple* was the one most likely to have produced a hostile response from black audiences. Although a number of black critics were harshly critical, Jacqueline Bobo, who researched the reactions of black women viewers of the film, reports that they were generally sympathetic to it.[12]

Films or movies?

Spielberg has always thought of film-making in terms of *mass* entertainment. From his earliest days as a film-maker, he expressed a desire to make films for large audiences. He told a school friend that 'movies were *the* great art form because they moved the most people ... he didn't want to play to an audience of the elite'.[13] As an established film-maker, his idea of the audience is very broad – 'It's pretty much everybody.' The apparent simplicity of this view of the audience disguises the enormous challenge it poses for a film-maker, especially one working in Hollywood at a time when the international audience was becoming commercially more important than the domestic one. It means making films for people who are divided by nationality, ethnicity, gender, age, class and cultural background.

Spielberg describes his relationship with the audience as 'pleasing' it. However, when he discusses the relationship in more detail, 'pleasing' doesn't seem the right word. The way he talks about *Jaws* provides a good example of why it doesn't:

> I chose to make a movie that would reach audiences really on two levels. The first level was a blow to the solar plexus, and the second was an upper cut, just under the nose; it was really a one–two, you're out, combination. I never intended anything deeper than that.[14]

Such an effect may not be deep but it's certainly strong! Conceived in such terms, the film-maker's relationship with his audience is an aggressive one, aimed at having an intense, visceral effect – 'I love to grip an audience and watch them lean forward in their seats or flinch at a wreck or at something frightening. I like involving the audience on a level of total participation.'[15]

However, as Spielberg's career has progressed, he has increasingly qualified his commitment to entertainment. He has suggested that film-making for entertainment isn't a fully mature activity. He believes that, as a film-maker grows older and takes on new responsibilities like marriage and family, he should make films that reflect this new state. Spielberg describes his own career as having developed from making 'fun' films like the *Indiana Jones* ones to 'serious' films like *Schindler's List*. 'Mature' film-making deals with serious and substantial social issues, which are dramatized in a sober way avoiding the techniques of entertainment. Discussing his approach to the making of *Schindler's List*, Spielberg said, 'It has to be accurate and it has to be fair and it cannot *in the least* come across as entertainment.'[16]

By describing a film-maker's development as a process of maturing, Spielberg appears to be making a qualitative distinction between two kinds of film-making. His description surely suggests that mature film-makers will make the best films. However, he never explicitly draws this conclusion and, as far as his own career is concerned, he argues for the right to make both kinds of films, as if they were equal in status.

The same issue comes up in another distinction Spielberg sometimes makes between *films* and *movies*. In a 1982 interview, he described Martin Scorsese as the best maker of *films* of their generation while George Lucas was the best maker of *movies*. The context of this comparison between Scorsese and Lucas is an illuminating one. He argues that (at that time) there were two groups of film-makers in Hollywood:

> I think the other group – Francis and Marty and some of the European film-makers – bring a lot of their urban development into their movies and take their films very seriously. They internalise who they are and express that on film. I think that if you put everybody together and rated them, Marty would have to be the best *film-maker* of our generation. George Lucas is the best *moviemaker*. You see, George and I have fun with our films. We don't take them as seriously.

Figure 4.2 Poster for *Indiana Jones and the Last Crusade*
(LucasFilm Ltd/Paramount/The Kobal Collection)

> And I think that our movies are about things that we think will appeal to other people, not just to ourselves. We think of ourselves first, but in the next breath we are talking about the audience and what works and what doesn't.[17]

On the face of it, Spielberg describes the two groups in an even-handed way: he doesn't appear to be suggesting that one is superior to the other. However, the terms he uses don't support this even-handedness. In contemporary criticism, films by people who are serious about their work and use it as a form of personal expression are highly valued as against films made by people who don't take their work so seriously and are preoccupied with audiences. There's a problem of vocabulary for somebody trying to give the two groups equal weight. There aren't terms to match the weight of 'serious' and 'personal expression'. 'Having fun' and 'thinking about the audience' suggest something lighter and more frivolous.

Pure entertainment

All of the films Spielberg has been associated with tend to raise general questions about the nature of entertainment. In a very direct and obvious way, the *Indiana Jones* trilogy (now a quartet with the arrival of *Indiana Jones and the Kingdom of the Crystal Skull*) raises the question of 'pure entertainment'. Is there such a thing? If a film obviously entertains audiences, is it possible to ignore the way it represents its characters and the social world they inhabit?

In interviews, both Spielberg and George Lucas discuss the trilogy as if it were an example of pure entertainment. For them, the four films have a simple ambition – to recreate the uncomplicated pleasures offered by the adventure stories of the 1930s and 1940s, the films of non-stop action built around the exploits of superheroes such as Zorro and Flash Gordon. Judged in those terms, the four films that make up the quartet are undeniably successful. Part archaeologist, part adventurer, Indiana Jones, with his bull whip, fedora and leather jacket, is a hero distinctive enough to join the company of Zorro, Flash Gordon, and the other superheroes who have left their mark on popular culture. In all four films, the film-makers provided him with varied and imaginative enough adventures to maintain the high level of dramatic excitement that is crucial to the success of films of this kind. The films are particularly successful in demonstrating how modern film-making techniques – sound, widescreen, visual effects – can be used without losing touch with the cheap, unpretentious feel of the films the trilogy is modelled on.

It's indicative of the low esteem that entertainment is held in that both Spielberg and Lucas tend to be defensive when they discuss the trilogy, despite its enormous success. Spielberg characterizes the films as 'popcorn movies' as if the pleasures they offered were insubstantial and short-lived. But this hardly a fair description of films which, twenty-odd years after they were made, can still produce responses like these:

> *Aaron 1375*: There are few movies I can watch over and over again, but this (*Raiders of the Lost Ark*) is one of them. This movie has it all: action, romance, comedy, and suspense. Harrison Ford is at his best as Dr. Jones, one of the most exciting archaeologists ever. From the start to the end you are hooked to this

movie. I love the opening when he has to dodge traps as he tries to get this treasure, I love it when he is running through the streets trying to save the girl, I just love every bit of it. Spielberg said he wanted a B-type movie like he remembered from his youth, but this far surpasses any B movie and any A movie as far as I am concerned.

Shawn Watson: *Temple of Doom* is, without a shadow of a doubt, the best Indiana Jones film. I know a lot of nerds are going to disagree with me but I do think it superior to *Raiders of the Lost Ark* because I prefer the darker, nastier tone and the fact that it just doesn't let up from the word 'go'! Two hours of *Temple of Doom*'s running time pass in a breeze of sheer adventure as Spielberg takes us from one memorable set-piece to another. The opening musical number, the fight in the Obi-Wan Club, the chase through Shanghai, the plane crash/dinghy ride, the journey to Pankot Palace, the dinner scene, the human sacrifice, the freeing of the slaves, the mine-cart ride, the water rush, the rope bridge, the cliff-hanging ... wow! How much more can you pack into a film? It's physically impossible!

Gottogorunning: When the two greatest film-makers in the world teamed up to create the best action movie of all time – *Raiders of the Lost Ark*, it seemed unlikely that they could duplicate their divinely-inspired work. After a miss with the entertaining yet forgettable Indiana Jones and the *Temple of Doom, Indiana Jones and the Last Crusade* comes pretty close to doing just that ... It is more abundant with humor than the previous two films, without the characters falling into irritating self-parody ... This film stands among the greatest action adventures of all time. I don't know anyone who hasn't seen it, but if you haven't, don't walk to see it. Run.[18]

These are hardly testimonies to experiences that have been insubstantial and short-lived!

However, this is not the whole of the story. The people who are most enthusiastic about the films usually ignore its political, social and gender dimensions. Set mainly in foreign lands, especially the Middle East, the trilogy invites objections to the way the countries and their inhabitants are portrayed. Edward Said's account of Orientalism has been challenged but the *Indiana Jones* trilogy would offer powerful evidence for anybody who wanted to bolster Said's position. Almost all the sins that Said attributes to Western accounts of the East can be found in the trilogy. In it, the East is an alien and mysterious terrain whose inhabitants are generally either passive spectators of the main action or threatening participants. Western academics (archaeologists) and soldiers range freely and unself-consciously across Eastern countries in search of sacred objects and treasures, which they take back to the West when they lay their hands on them.

The trilogy is similarly open to feminist objections. *Raiders of the Lost Ark* begins promisingly with Marion Ravenwood as an unexpectedly aggressive character who is central to the action but, as the film progresses she becomes more of a secondary character, the woman in need of protection. 'Willie' Scott in *Indiana Jones and the Temple of Doom* is, throughout the film, a secondary character, incapacitated by her femininity. In *Indiana Jones and the Last Crusade*, Elsa Schneider is more active but, in the tradition of the James Bond films, is the familiar female character who combines sexual attractiveness with duplicity.

Are criticisms of this kind beside the point? The films clearly don't offer themselves as serious commentaries on international politics or the position of women. Shouldn't they be discussed as the light-hearted entertainments they're intended to be? Contemporary cultural critics have generally been unsympathetic to such defences, arguing that, whatever their makers' intentions, the way films represent the social world and its inhabitants is too important to be ignored. There's no such thing as innocent entertainment.

In his discussion of the trilogy, Joseph McBride forcefully expresses this position:

> In their portraits of the Third World heavies, Spielberg and Lucas fall into the trap of uncritically imitating antiquated Hollywood conventions. But the absence of malicious intent hardly excuses the presence of such stereotypes in movies made in the 1980s; indeed, one can argue that their unthinking perpetuation for the purposes of mass entertainment constitutes a far more insidious form of racial insult. With its revival of previously discredited fantasies of American cultural dominance over Third World primitives and cartoonish villains from an evil empire, *Raiders of the Lost Ark* was the perfect film to mark the beginning of the Reagan era.[19]

McBride's account of the film is itself rather heavy-handed. The principal 'heavies' in the film are French and German and for at least half the film the conflict at the centre of the action is exclusively between Indiana Jones and the German army. And stereotyping isn't confined to Third World characters – Marcus Brody is an English stereotype, the army officers are German ones, and, for that matter, Indiana Jones is an American one. Stereotyping is used as a way of representing characters for comic effect.

Although it needs refining, we agree with McBride's criticism. But we don't want to judge the film only in his terms. We believe that the responses of the large number of fans who greatly enjoyed the films shouldn't be ignored. When describing their responses, they generally ignore the social and political attitudes that are represented in the film. For them, other things are more important. The first response that we quoted captures very well what those things are when the writer says, 'This movie has it all: action, romance, comedy, and suspense.' For all its innocence, we agree with this claim just as much as we do with McBride's criticism. The films display an energy and inventiveness that are exhilarating. They demonstrate many of the basic appeals of the cinema, the kinds of qualities that have made it so successful as a form of mass entertainment. Because entertainment is so often defined as a superficial experience, its quality is frequently ignored and a film is judged on the basis of its political and social shortcomings. This seems to us the wrong way round. Films aren't principally commentaries on the social and political world. They certainly express social and political attitudes but they have other qualities which are just as, or even more, important.

The makers of the *Indiana Jones* trilogy do deserve criticism in this area although of a rather different kind. Their ambition was to remake the serials of the 1930s and 1940s but with a contemporary sensibility and technique. George Lucas explained that when he and Spielberg first viewed the films that had excited them as youngsters, 'I was appalled at how I could have been so enthralled with something so bad. And I said, "Holy smokes, if I

Figure 4.3 *Schindler's List*
(Universal/The Kobal Collection)

got excited about this stuff, it's going to be easy for me to get kids excited about the same thing only better." '[20]

Lucas and Spielberg approached most of the conventions of the older films with an energy and imagination that certainly made them better. But their approach was uneven: there are areas of the films where they are content to rely on old conventions and the film is less vibrant. In particular, they too easily rely on the long-established convention that the Orient represents mystery and threat.

Although it is set in South America rather than the Orient, the opening of *Raiders of the Lost Ark* is a very good example of the problem. As Indy and his assistants walk through the jungle to the caves where the treasure they seek is located, sound and light are used very effectively to create sense of a dense and inhospitable environment. The soundscape that Ben Burtt creates, with its wide range of distinct and unsettling sounds, is especially important for creating a sense of imminent danger. The writer and the production designer then show a fertile imagination in the number and character of the traps they create for Indy to avoid before he can get the treasure and escape from the cave. All of this is exhilarating film-making. But the creation of character is much more uneven. As we've already suggested, the character of Indy with his whip, fedora and leather jacket is an engaging riff on the traditional hero. But his assistants, whose ethnic identity isn't well defined except that they aren't white and Anglo-Saxon, are much less freshly imagined. They are defined by predictable attributes in that they are fearful and untrustworthy. And the film-makers even commit the cardinal sin of having an English actor play the most prominent role. And when Indy disposes of them, a threatening group with bows and arrows, who appear to have been transposed from a Western, confronts him.

The occasional acceptance of old outmoded conventions certainly limits all four films. However, it doesn't seriously undermine them. As the audience responses we've quoted indicate, it's the fresh and imaginative way the basic conventions of the genre are handled that has the strongest impact.

The limits of mass entertainment

A director whose name had become synonymous with mass entertainment makes a film about the Holocaust – *Schindler's List* is a key film for anybody interested in what's possible within mass entertainment. One of the early reviewers of the film, John Gross, described the issues the film provokes very clearly,

> Suppose the Disney organization announced that it was planning a film about the Holocaust. Better still, suppose Walt Disney himself had, thirty or forty years back. In common fairness, we would have had to wait and see how it all worked out; but common sense would have suggested heavy misgivings. The gap between the Disney tradition and the demands of the material would simply have seemed too wide to be bridged.
>
> Something of the same doubts stole into my mind when I heard that Steven Spielberg was finally making his long-deferred film of *Schindler's List*. Disney was the greatest popular entertainer of his time. Spielberg is his closest contemporary equivalent. Such words are not to be lightly spoken; they argue a kind of genius.

> *But popular entertainment has its limits, and anything you can profitably say about the Holocaust – except, perhaps, at the level of simple lessons for children – lies well beyond them.*[21] (Our italics)

Given this description, Gross's judgment of the film comes as a surprise: 'In the event my fears, or the worst of them, were altogether misplaced. The skills are there, certainly, but Spielberg also shows a firm moral and emotional grasp of his material. The film is an outstanding achievement.' When Gross goes on to discuss the nature of that achievement, he acknowledges that the film is working within the conventions of mass entertainment:

> It is also a straightforward piece of storytelling. Whether or not its box-office takings eventually rival those of *ET* or *Jurassic Park*, it is also accessible to a mass audience. No previous American movie treatment of the Holocaust (certainly not *Sophie's Choice*, still less, the dire *Holocaust* itself) comes anywhere near to it, but in its energy and confident popular approach it is still a recognizable product of Hollywood.[22]

Not everybody agreed that it was possible to dramatize the Holocaust within the conventions of mass entertainment in an acceptable way. Predictably, Jean Luc-Godard attacked the film on these grounds. One of the reasons he gave for refusing an honour from the New York Film Critics' Circle was the failure of the group 'to prevent Mr Spielberg reconstructing Auschwitz'. In a collection of essays about the film, Miriam Hansen offers a more articulate version of this position. For her, Spielberg's project was doomed from the start because:

> *Schindler's List* is and remains a Hollywood product. As such, it is circumscribed by the economic and ideological tenets of the culture industry, with its unquestioned and supreme values of entertainment and spectacle, its fetishism of style and glamour ... Since the business of Hollywood is entertainment, preferably in the key of sentimental optimism, there is something intrinsically and profoundly incommensurable about 're-creating' the traumatic effects of the Shoah 'for the sake of audiences' recreation'.[23]

What is most striking about this judgment of the film is Hansen's evident distaste for mass entertainment. In expressing that distaste, she writes within a very recognizable discourse. Entertainment is identified in familiar terms as 'spectacle, style, glamour and sentimental optimism'. It's judged negatively because it is embedded within the values of the culture industry. As the reference to the culture industry suggests, Hansen's position has its roots in the ideas of the Frankfurt School. This isn't the place for a full engagement with that position. At this point, we will limit our objections to saying that it leads into the aesthetic ghetto of avant-garde art and to political impotence (a situation so depressingly inhabited by Godard).

We don't want to claim that there aren't problems about making a film that deals with the Holocaust within the conventions of mass entertainment. Spielberg was certainly aware of many of those problems. John H. Richardson has provided an illuminating account of the making of the film which reveals how Spielberg's concern created tensions at a basic level of film-making. Spielberg told Richardson, 'The authenticity of the story was too important to fall back on the commercial techniques that had gotten me a certain reputation in the area of craft and polish.' He went on to describe his approach: 'I threw a whole bunch of tools out of the toolbox. One of them was a crane. One of them was colour film. I just limited the utensils, so the story would be the strength of the piece. There's nothing flashy in this movie at all.' But then Richardson adds that Spielberg paused, before saying, 'I hope it's not too dull.'

A little later, Richardson describes Spielberg at work:

> He considers using a dolly. He tucks his chin in and stares at the ground. His baseball cap comes down at an oblique angle to his nose, like a resting bird. 'The dolly shot would be a real Hollywood shot,' he says, 'a real movie shot on a normal "movie" movie.' On a movie like this, a pan is always the choice. ... He decides to go for a longer lens to get more of the crowd in the picture – but not too long. 'A little closer and I can justify hearing the dialogue,' he says. 'And when they start walking it justifies a dolly.'
>
> Having changed his mind, he orders up a dolly track.[24]

The tension between choosing the right approach and making a dull film isn't only evident in decisions about how to shoot the film. It's evident in other areas. An examination of the way the film is adapted from Thomas Keneally's novel is helpful in this respect as it highlights where other tensions occur and how they are resolved. Although it's a work of fiction, the novel has a strong foundation in historical fact. Much of its appeal depends on a claim to authenticity. Keneally drew heavily on the memoirs of the survivors and other documentary evidence for his narrative. He claims not to have invented anything, apart from reconstructing conversations between characters – there haven't been any serious challenges to his claim. There's a very close relationship between novel and film. The only source for the script appears to have been the novel: there's no evidence that Steven Zaillian and Spielberg used any other sources. In adapting the novel, Zaillian did a remarkable job, deftly encompassing its overall perspective, most of the characters, and the many and varied events it describes. He made some changes: adding a few invented scenes and altering the details of some events. Although none of these changes is major, they do reveal the way he and Spielberg coped with their anxiety about boring the audience.

Some of the changes are clearly designed to strengthen what humour there is in the story. The way Schindler raises capital to fund his business provides one good example of how this is achieved. In the novel, Keneally deals with the event matter-of-factly and indirectly. The reader is simply told that Adam Bankier (the original manager of the factory who is now working for Schindler) contacts Jews he knows and persuades them to invest on the understanding that they'll receive a regular supply of the factory's output. The fact that the men know Bankier provides them with some assurance that Schindler will keep his side of the bargain. In the film, the action is dramatized in two invented scenes. In the first, Schindler asks Izhak Stern to make contacts for raising money. The scene is given a comic touch by Schindler's brazen declaration – when asked by Stern what he will offer in return for the money – that his contribution will be his presentation skills. The second scene is more strongly comic but works in a similar way, highlighting Oscar as a charming rogue. Stern brings two men to Schindler's car. The two characters are lightly drawn stereotypes of Jewish businessmen: small, old men, suspicious and determined to drive a hard bargain. The scene develops as a classic comic reversal – Schindler charmingly overcoming their innate caution by forcing them to see they have no alternative but to accept his terms, even though they have no guarantee that he will keep his side of the bargain.

This isn't an example of real events being distorted by the desire to entertain. In the novel, Keneally doesn't just present the unvarnished truth: he has his own strategies for entertaining his readers. In his account of these events, he uses one of classic ways realist novelists engage readers, through the representation of a dense social world. His representation has extra dramatic interest because the world is in crisis. How Schindler takes advantage of this crisis to manipulate things in his favour is, of course, one of the ways that Keneally develops his character.

The changes that Zaillian/Spielberg made don't go against the grain of the novel, which has a number of comic touches. Most of those are transferred directly to the film. In general, the comic scenes are written and directed in a low-key, controlled way. The only sequence which writer and director seriously misjudge is the audition for the post of Schindler's secretary. The humour, which is provoked by either the incompetence or the ugliness of the women, is tired and obvious.

The characterization of Schindler creates the most difficulties for Spielberg, given his anxiety about entertaining the audience without compromising the film. The actual Oscar Schindler wasn't a conventional hero. He behaved heroically during the Holocaust but his motives for doing so remain mysterious. His career and personal behaviour, both before and after the war, give no clues as to why he took such risks during it. In significant ways, especially his treatment of his wife (and other women), he was an unattractive man. Even the people closest to him, like his wife and the Jews he saved, have been unable to account for his wartime behaviour. So a novel or a film that wants to claim authenticity has to respect the mystery and avoid portraying him as a conventional hero.

For Keneally, the problem wasn't so difficult because his authorial position is at a distance from the events he narrates. The novel has two dimensions: narration and commentary. Keneally describes Schindler's actions while at the same time discussing the problems of understanding his motivation. Even then, Schindler emerges from the novel as something of a romantic hero: a flamboyant risk taker and attractive to women. For the film-makers, the challenge was a bigger one since the romantic hero is an iconic character in entertainment cinema. The script doesn't hide Schindler's flaws: his betrayal of his wife, for example, is directly and sharply dramatized. And in both the writing and the acting, there are suggestions that Schindler was an opportunist who traded on his charm.

Other features of the film encourage a romantic view. Although Liam Neeson's performance is generally excellent, his physical presence – he's fair, tall and rangy, with strongly defined features – is that of a conventional hero. And the images in the opening of the film, with their low angles and close-ups of Schindler's face in profile, emphasize his heroic characteristics. At the end of the film, both writing and direction add to the heroic emphasis. Although Schindler's announcement of the end of the war to a large audience of his Jewish employees and their Nazi guards is true to the facts, the scene is directed in a way that highlights the theatricality of the situation and Schindler's authoritative command of it. And in the next scene, he breaks down, saying he could have saved many more Jews. The scene, which is an invention by the writer, adds to Schindler's heroic status by adding pathos to it.

There are other points in the film where similar problems to the ones we've been discussing are evident. A familiar connection between Nazi violence and classical music is made in a scene where a German officer plays the piano in the midst of the murderous liquidation of the ghetto. And the characterization of Ammon Goth draws on another (over-) familiar way of presenting the Nazis, in terms of perverse violence and sexuality. But even if all these issues are added together, we don't believe that they amount to evidence of a fundamentally misjudged approach in the treatment of the Holocaust. Before any final estimate of *Schindler's List* can be made, its successes, as well as its problems, need to be acknowledged – as does the relationship of those successes to the conventions of mass entertainment.

Let's take as an example one of the film's major successes, the delineation of the larger context in which Schindler's actions take place. That context is the displacement of the Krakow Jews as they are expelled from their homes to the ghetto, from the ghetto to a labour camp, and finally from the labour camp to an extermination camp. The displacement involves the movement of hundreds of people, on foot, by train, and by lorry. Sometimes, the movement is slow and orderly, sometimes it is chaotic and violent, sometimes people collaborate, and sometimes they resist. As well as a physical displacement, it's also an emotional one because most of the Jews are moving towards their deaths.

To dramatize such a complex phenomenon, Spielberg drew on his proven ability to create spectacle. This may seem a misguided way of praising the film since spectacle, in recent film criticism, has strongly negative connotations, suggesting a phenomenon with a superficially attractive surface behind which there is no substance. But this is a particular use of the word, part of the anti-mass entertainment discourse – it's no accident that Miriam Hansen cites spectacle as one of Hollywood's vices. Outside of this discourse, spectacle has positive connotations as well as negative ones. Indeed, many of the cinema's triumphs, from *Battleship Potemkin* to *House of Flying Daggers,* have been achieved through the creation of spectacle. The liquidation of the ghetto in *Schindler's List* demonstrates how staging, composition, camera movement, editing and sound can be used to create spectacle that is powerful enough to represent some of the terrors of the Holocaust.

If there is a problem with the film, it's because Spielberg's approach bears the marks of some defensiveness, created by his anxiety about the status of entertainment. That defensiveness is evident in his early declaration that *Schindler's List* shouldn't come across as an entertainment. Having said what the film *shouldn't* come across as, Spielberg didn't go on to say what it *should* come across as. Because there isn't a positive view, the challenge – to avoid possible clichés and stereotypes – is sometimes met by a low-key use of those clichés and stereotypes rather than new inventions. In his review of *Schindler's List*, John Gross claimed that mass entertainment has limits which can't accommodate an intelligent account of the Holocaust. But in praising the film and acknowledging that it is 'a very recognisable product of Hollywood', he created a significant contradiction in his position. If the mass entertainment tradition can accommodate films that 'show a firm moral and emotional grasp' of the Holocaust, then it's hard to imagine what issues couldn't be accommodated. Anything seems possible.

The end

Critics frequently identify *Schindler's List* as the film which marks a radical change in Steven Spielberg's career, the film which demonstrates his move from lightweight entertainer to serious artist. As we already noted, Spielberg often describes the development of his career in this way. But, as Peter Kramer has suggested, this is a misleading account. *Schindler's List* was far from being the first 'serious' film that Spielberg directed. *The Color Purple* and *Empire of the Sun* would certainly have to be included as 'serious' films. But it's not really a matter of arguing about which films are 'serious' and which are 'fun'. The division itself needs to be challenged if Spielberg's career is to be properly understood. His career is better described as an imaginative exploration of the entire mass entertainment tradition. We can learn a great deal about the strengths and limits of that tradition from the films he's made, the *Indiana Jones* films just as much as *Schindler's List*.

5 The perspective of entertainers
Interviews with film-makers

Seeing and hearing the first *Star Wars* movie pushed me over the edge. It was such a paradigm shift. A huge number of people got their chromosomes rear-ranged by watching that film, and that's what made me decide to push ahead doing movie sound.

(Randy Thom)[1]

The moment that the whole idea of filmmaking hit me was when I was 15 and went to see *The Seventh Seal*. I'd seen lots of movies before that, of course – the average number of films a kid growing up in New York City would see. But *The Seventh Seal* was the film where I suddenly understood the concept that some-body made this film, and that there was a series of decisions that could have been different if someone else had made the film. I really got a sense of a single person's interest and passions through watching that film, which in fact was true. This was Ingmar Bergman, after all.

(Walter Murch)[2]

Film-makers are rarely asked questions concerning their views and feelings about the nature of their job. When they are, questions usually revolve around issues concerning their responsibility towards the large audiences that the films to which they contribute are capable of reaching and, potentially at least, influence. Even rarer are questions that probe film-makers' views of their role as entertainers. Given the nature of our project, we felt it was important to add this perspective to our exploration of the relationship between art and entertainment in the cinema. To this end, we talked to several industry professionals in Hollywood in the Spring of 2007.[3]

One of the most common criticisms of entertainment is that, while it may offer a sense of the spectacular, it remains 'mindless', thus operating as an inhibitor of intel-lectual and critical functions, a sort of sleep of consciousness embellished by an exalta-tion of the senses. What, then, are we to make of those film-makers (and there are hundreds of them) who are primarily responsible for what we come to define as enter-tainment? Are they simply clogs in an unthinking, uncaring machine aimed at max-imizing profit while minimizing risk? If they are not, what do they actually think about what they do? Are their views on entertainment and art in any way revealing of their own attitudes to cinema and film-making?

For logistical reasons, we chose to focus on film-makers who have made their home and professional base in the Bay Area, that is, San Francisco and vicinity. Not only have most of the key films in contemporary cinema originated from or been influenced by film-makers living and working in the Bay Area (from *The Godfather* to *Star Wars* and from

Raiders of the Lots Ark to *Toy Story*); this is also an area that has witnessed some of the most significant developments that have shaped the film industry in terms of both new production facilities and creative enterprises (Zoetrope, Lucasfilm, Pixar) as well as new technologies that have revolutionized the ways films are made and experienced (Dolby, THX, Renderman).[4]

Two individuals among those whom we interviewed ultimately stood out as particularly significant to this project. Randy Thom and Walter Murch have been in the industry for several decades and have been part of most of the changes and breakthroughs highlighted above, sometimes from the very privileged position of being able to action change. Multiple Oscar winners both, their backgrounds, experience of the industry and films they have worked on make them very interesting film-makers to focus on.[5] Murch and Thom have worked with directors such as Francis Ford Coppola, George Lucas, Steven Spielberg, Robert Zemeckis, Anthony Minghella, Tim Burton and David Lynch.[6] Among the films they have worked on are *American Graffiti*, *The Godfather*, *Apocalypse Now*, *Star Wars* and many others. In particular, we thought that the dynamics of their backgrounds and long-term friendship – Murch gave Thom his first job on *Apocalypse Now* – made them very interesting case studies. Since they have worked together in the past, and in view of their long-term relationship with effectively the 'who's who' of Hollywood cinema, their approaches and attitudes to art and entertainment are very interesting and, we hope, revealing.

Cultural beginnings

Murch and Thom could not have had more different upbringings in cultural terms. Walter Murch was born in New York. His father, Walter Tandy Murch, was a respected painter, primarily influenced by Impressionism and Surrealism, and whose interests in high art and music (especially the violin) were to play a major role in the cultural upbringing and interest of his son. Murch senior's engagement with a variety of art forms and their popular application (his most popular work is arguably represented by the covers he created for *Scientific American*) ensured that Walter Murch junior was exposed from a very early age to the life of artists and their work.[7] Murch attended USC's film school, arguably the most prestigious film school in the USA and what was at the time a hotbed of innovation and new creative talent.[8] It was there that he formed key creative partnerships, first, with George Lucas, later, through Lucas himself, with Francis Ford Coppola, who gave Murch his first job on *The Rainy People* in 1969. This was the beginning of a long-term friendship and professional collaboration between Murch and Coppola. When Coppola and Lucas decided to move away from Los Angeles and traditional Hollywood modes of production to settle north in the San Francisco Bay Area, Murch followed and was one of the key players in sowing the seeds for what is now known as Bay Area cinema. In particular, Murch worked with Coppola in establishing Zoetrope as a new production company. Although Murch is well known as a film editor, he is also universally acknowledged as one of the fathers, with Ben Burtt, another USC graduate, of contemporary film sound.

Randy Thom was born in Shreveport, Louisiana, literally a corporate town created by the Shreve Town Company in the late nineteenth century. Significantly for Thom's future career, the city became known for a radio programme, *The Louisiana Hayride*, which got its nickname 'the Cradle of the Stars' mainly because it helped launch the careers of many innovative popular musicians of the 1950s and 1960s, including Elvis Presley. Radio was indeed to play a central role in Thom's formative years. While a student at Antioch College in the early 1970s, Thom joined WYSO radio, a college radio station that would eventually spawn several industry professionals. The exploratory nature of the work carried out at WYSO shaped Thom's creative identity, as well as alerting him to the importance of collaboration: 'Antioch was the place where people explored things and tried their best to break new ground. And I think that sometimes you are lucky and you get an organisation an institution like WYSO that not only attracts people like that but also mixes them together in a certain kind of way.'[9]

Thom eventually moved west to Berkeley, California, where he worked as a producer at KPFA, one of the most significant radio stations of the West Coast.[10] It was during this time that he grew increasingly conscious of the work that new sound men and women working in films had started experimenting with. Finally, a phone call to Walter Murch led to his first job on *Apocalypse Now*.

Both Murch and Thom have worked on a remarkably varied number of films and other projects. The scope and breadth of their work place them directly at the epicentre of what we today call contemporary Hollywood cinema.

Film-makers as entertainers

Our first question to Thom and Murch was inevitable: do they see themselves as entertainers?

RANDY THOM (RT hereon): I do think I'm an entertainer. I'd like to think of myself as an artist too, and I don't think that the two things are mutually exclusive. I think certainly when I work in feature films my job is to entertain. I think really top-notch entertainment is not simply aimed at occupying people's minds or giving them an opportunity to forget their troubles. It also raises interesting questions in people's minds, whether those questions occur to them while they're watching the film or later is irrelevant in some ways I think, and it has the potential to change people's lives as well. I think that's the most difficult entertainment of all to pull off. When I think of films that do that, I think of films like *The Godfather*, for instance, which you can easily view on a fairly superficial level as a gangster movie and find it very entertaining, but it also contains loads of information about American culture and politics, etc. Though there isn't anything about it that was absolutely

WALTER MURCH (WM hereon): ground-breaking, I think it did push certain envelopes and bend certain rules in interesting ways, and I think that's always a good thing to do in any kind of entertainment or art. Yes, if you allow that word to be an expansive as possible. Anyone who works on something that allows large amounts of strangers to assemble in the dark to watch what they do has to be an entertainer and has to have some element of the circus about it, there is a circus-type element. 'Come and see something you've never seen before, this way gentleman, it's starting at eight o'clock, you'll definitely get your money's worth ... and the young lady as well. Please come this way!' We do that in refined and sometimes not so refined ways, but we all do it. So, yes, I think applies to everybody. Once you or everyone who works in motion pictures or television or whatever you call this, that is changing and emerging.

In both Murch's and Thom's case there is a clear awareness of their role as entertainers but this is mixed from the onset with a rather strong sense of ambivalence about it. Interestingly, both introduce important qualifications to their statements. Thom articulates his position by referring to 'top-notch entertainment' and films that 'push certain envelopes and bend certain rules in interesting ways' whereas Murch speaks of doing entertainment in 'refined and sometimes not so refined ways'. They also seem to suggest that *all* film-makers are entertainers. Overall, their words seem aimed at shortening the distance between art and entertainment. Thom, in particular, does this in identifying *The Godfather* as an example of films capable of working on both a superficial level and a deeper one. It is also significant, however, that neither commits entirely to the idea of being thought of solely as entertainers. Both are rather careful in highlighting that though they may be happy to be called entertainers, they understand their contribution as going beyond 'pure' entertainment. Where does this reluctance come from?

RT: Well, I suspect that there is this belief that entertaining is this superficial thing, and none of us want to be superficial. You could say the same sort of thing about certain genres of painting. There are certain kinds of painting that are thought to be pretty.

There's an American painter, Thomas Kinkade, who does very idyllic landscapes of villages and cottages, and is widely negatively critiqued by people who say that it's just a pretty picture. It may be quite difficult from a technical point of view to make that picture because it involves figuring out how to display three dimensions in two and working out colours, etc. But then people will say that it doesn't say to me anything other than just a delightful image. Most of us who engage in entertainment, however you define that, have the same kind of ambivalence about it.[11]

Thom articulates here what remains a central concern for film-makers, namely that the concept of technique, so central to professional discourses of craftsmanship and skill, might need to be downgraded in relation to some other, as yet undefined, 'higher' artistic quality. Does this concern about the perceived 'lightness' of entertainment impact on the way in which Thom and Murch approach film projects? We asked Thom this question in relation to two films he has worked on, *Arlington Road* and *The Incredibles*: did he approach these two films with any different degree of attention because one is about terrorism and the other one is about a family of superheroes?

> RT: No. I think it's because I'm so well trained at this point to be concerned about my client, I guess. My main mission when I'm working is to make my client happy, which is the director of the film, the producer of the film that I'm working on. I may have my own personal agenda, I may agree with or not agree with the themes of the film, but I'm enough of a so-called professional, whether that's a good thing or a bad thing, that I'm able to push that aside and do as good a job that I'm capable of at that time on that film.

While Thom emphasizes the professional nature of his approach to film-making as the key to his attitudes towards different projects, Murch chooses to historicize this issue in relation to other art forms: why has entertainment historically been understood as different and ultimately less meaningful than art? Why this split?

> WM: I think that that's an unfortunate side effect of certain trends that happened in the twentieth century. I think if you looked from the nineteenth century on back, you wouldn't find such a split. The exact reasons for that split are a book unto themselves, but there was in painting and in the novel and in music at the beginning of the twentieth century, there was almost a conscious abandonment of subject matter, story and melody the way we understand it, and these are things that allow entertainment to happen, in the largest sense of the word. The great artists of the ancient world, and of the Renaissance, and of China did not abandon these things, but there was this split, which I think had something to do with the trauma of the First World War and the cultural reaction to that. It was the feeling of a kind of abandonment, that the nineteenth century had seemed so promising and then it led to this carnage, therefore everything about the nineteenth century is wrong and we have to invent new ways, because we don't want this to happen again. On the other hand, what we found was that that decision led almost directly to the Second World War and the Cold War. So we're still as a culture reverberating from those things, but I think that one of the side effects was this splitting of art and entertainment. Not least of which was the emergence right at that time of this seventh art, cinema, which was obviously a popular art because, and economically, it required large audiences to support it. There were various attempts by people to pull cinema into the fine art area, but looked at broadly as a cultural

phenomenon, that's just a tiny slice of the enterprise. So, I think quite early on film, because it was new and not understood, because it had no tradition obviously, and because it did require early on millions of people, it became classified as entertainment. It's not that there isn't artistry within it, but the artistry peeks out at you from strange places within the film, in places that you might not expect.

Here Murch demonstrates a rather developed awareness of the cultural debate around the importance of cinema as a mass medium and of the arguments against its mass appeal. Interestingly, although he calls the split between art and entertainment an 'unfortunate side effect' he does not promote a different, possibly more positive view of cinema. While he seems to be getting to grips with the heart of the problem, Murch seems to suggest the existence of a difference between cinema and other art forms that manifests itself in the ways in which quality, defined here as artistry, emerges in films from 'strange places, in places you might not expect'. Unfortunately, he does not elaborate upon the notion of artistry.

Murch's words offer a good lead into discussing issues concerning industry-wide attitudes to entertainment. Do film-makers truly perceive cinema as a different art form from painting or literature in terms of its relationship to entertainment? And is this the result of external pressures or are film-makers part of the 'problem'?

WM: Something struck me two years ago, maybe it was *The Aviator* and the comment in the article [I read] said that Marty [Martin Scorsese] was still 'fiddling with the film'. He was making these fine incremental touches to it, but as far as the journalist or whoever wrote the article was concerned, that was dithering, it was insignificant and by implication, possibly destructive, worrying, 'Come on Marty, just show us the film!'. There is an impatience with the detail or a lack of understanding of the importance of the detail, but in fact, one's whole response to a film or anything, a book, etc., can be spoiled by one wrong word in the wrong place, that makes you suddenly question everything that the author wrote. How can he put that word there? If it isn't right, we throw the book away. We have those similar things ... I think it's partly that question of survivability over time, these things that we're making are hopefully little boats being launched into the ocean of the future and we don't know what storms or weather they will encounter because we don't know what the world is going to be like in the future, but we're trying our best to protect them and to give them the right bone structure and the right sustenance and the right skin that will serve them well and universalize them as much as possible so that when they're looked at fifty or a hundred years from now, people can respond to them. On the other hand, what this journalist was talking about in terms of 'fiddling' was 'give me my hamburger, I'm hungry right now!' and Marty, he's still in the back flipping the burger for the tenth time, just 'give me my hamburger!' It's a consumable, it's the difference and the film's both. It is something that you consume but for those of us that work on it, it's also something that we feel we have an obligation to protect into the future, and that attention to detail is one of the ways as you rightly put it, it's not just us, writers do it, painters do it, musicians do it, and it is seen as a valuable thing when they do it but I think because of this, the consumable nature of film, that it is a mass medium.

Murch's words are interesting in many ways but two aspects stand out. First, he does not query the basic nature of the accusation: film-making is, at least in part, guilty of being a consumable. His words would appear to suggest that this is the result of outside pressures (the press, ignorance about film-making, etc.) rather than internal issues pertaining to film-makers' own attitudes. Second, Murch seems to appropriate discourses of crafts-manship, skill, patience and time in ways that are typical of other, presumed higher art forms, namely painting and literature. Conversely, when Thom approached this subject, his reply implicates film-makers more directly:

> RT: In recent years, I've worked on quite a few animated films, and people tend to think of animated films as cartoons. It's funny that within the film-making community, especially within the animated film-making community, the word cartoon is almost a curse word these days. It's funny that everybody has this deep reverence, for instance, for the sound of the Warner Brothers cartoons of the forties, fifties and sixties. Virtually no director of an animated film these days would dream of allowing me to create sounds similar to those, because the drive in contemporary animated films seems to be in most cases pushing them in the direction of sounding like live-action films. I wonder if that even is a response to this idea of animated films being superficial, purely entertainment, and these film-makers don't want to make things that are purely superficial and entertainment. They want to make things that are entertaining and are also meaningful, and maybe you can't be meaningful if you have 'whoopy cushion' sounds and 'boings'.

Clearly, Thom is directly invoking industry-wide attitudes to entertainment as being responsible not merely for unspoken views of entertainment but directly accountable for film-making practices. If Thom is correct here, and the evidence from recent animated films supports his claim, concerns about entertainment and its lack of 'weight', far from being secondary or inconsequential, are actually integral to the decisions film-makers make in the creative process and how this then translates into production practices.

How then do film-makers 'professionalize' these concerns and questions about their role as entertainers? In particular, are film-makers any clearer as to the difference, if any, between 'pure' entertainment and 'serious' entertainment? Throughout our book the latter notion, namely the possibility of identifying something that could be defined as pure entertainment, has proved an elusive concept. Are film-makers any clearer on what one can identify as entertainment pure and simple and is there any such a thing, in their view? When asked, the concept of professionalism and operational expertise resurfaces yet again:

RT: I'd say that if it were possible to do a film that was purely entertainment, it wouldn't necessarily be an easy thing to do. For instance, making people laugh is often a very difficult thing to do. Some actor, whose name I've forgotten, who I think was on his deathbed, was asked: 'Is it hard to die?' He replied, 'No, death is easy, comedy is difficult.' As an actor he had found comedy the most difficult job he'd tackled. I think you could say the same thing about comedy in most forms, and comedy probably more than most forms tends to be thought of as entertainment.

I think what either the audience or the film-maker might refer to as pure entertainment is not necessarily easy to create. I think it's very often extremely difficult to create an experience that the audience can receive as simple, flowing and unencumbered, because there are all sorts of structural problems that, if you think of making a film, for instance, as a construction project, making the analogy to building a skyscraper, and there are many analogies actually because they cost about the same and can take about the same length of time. There are all kinds of unanticipated road blocks that you run into in telling a film story.

Thom believes also that this is a fundamental aspect that runs currently throughout the industry, into decisions made by the Academy and the Guilds:

RT: The *Star Wars* films have fallen victim to the same attitude. Some people are critical of John Williams' scores in the *Star Wars* films, and I think they have no idea how difficult it was for him or for anybody to come up with those themes that worked that well for those first three *Star Wars* films. So, I think because it's an action adventure, because it's a fantasy, people tend to take it lightly and think that because it flows over me in an easy way, it must have been easy to produce, and they're entirely wrong about that.

Thom refers to *Star Wars*, undoubtedly one of the films of our era that have succeeded in merging technology with storytelling and this introduces this crucial relationship into the debate about art and entertainment. The relationship with technology and its effects on creativity has been at the centre of so much debate concerning popular culture at large and film-making in particular. Are film-makers aware of this debate and of its correlated variation, the distinction between artists and technicians and its unavoidable association that the former deal with art, the latter deal with technology?

WM: Yes, there are film-makers who think that, there certainly was when we, Francis [Coppola], George [Lucas] and I left Los Angeles to start Zoetrope Studios up here [San Francisco], it was a reaction against people who thought that way, because we were very interested in technology and how technology could help us to tell different stories through the technology. Also to use emerging technology to allow us to make films less expensively in an environment where that would be possible, and it didn't seem to be possible in the studio-structured system in Los Angeles, which was organized differently. So, we shifted ecosystems where we could use this new technology and use it in multi-disciplinary ways and in many ways and the seeds of Industrial Light and Magic were born out of that, and also the emergence of what we call now 5.1 sound came out of that, and lots of smaller developments that all fit into those streams, for instance, different ways of editing. We were one of the first groups in America to use the European flatbed editing systems, starting in the late sixties. So, when you talk to me about these things, partly because I can be seen as a technician and do a lot of technical things, but also because the film-makers who I grew up with and who I live with on a daily basis are people who also believe what I do. You know, Francis is that way, George is that way and most of the film-makers I know in San Francisco area think that way.

Murch qualifies further his statement by discussing *Jurassic Park* and its contribution to cinema:

WM: Certainly, the art in *Jurassic Park* without question was the emergence of the digital creature. That was the first time that three-dimensional digital beings strolled about the stage, and it interacted with human beings in a complex and emotional and primal instinctual way, to the extent that it was completely believable to the audience and that's as significant a development as gesso as a form of painting. It allows a freedom of expression that was not possible prior to that, and Steve [Spielberg] showed that it could be done, and that it could reap huge economical benefits. A sidelight to that relates back to what we were talking about earlier, is that he went into doing *Jurassic Park* thinking that he would have to do it with stop motion models and with puppets. It was a team at Industrial Light and Magic who said, I think we can do it; there was scepticism but the team asked to do a test. So they did the test and Spielberg saw that it was possible, and he said 'Let's do it.' So it wasn't that the film director had said that they were going to break new ground, it was just the opposite. The film-maker obviously knows as much about the technical possibilities of a film as anyone, and he was hesitant going into that, and even privately hesitant to the extent that he thought 'How can we do this well, obviously we're going to have to do it in stop motion like they did in *The Empire Strikes Back*?', and when doing close-up work they would have thought they would do some puppetry like they did in *Jaws*. Yet out of the collective work of the film-makers emerged that this discovery which is a significant artistic breakthrough.

As Murch does above, Thom also chooses to highlight the collaborative nature of the film-making process. His words actually go to the very heart of another issue we have discussed in this book and that permeates arguments concerning the difference between art and entertainment, namely authorial agency. Curiously, though not surprisingly, he does so by borrowing an analogy from Murch:

RT: I think that Walter Murch once made the analogy to a new battleship that had just been commissioned, and on the first morning that the battleship leaves the port it's written down exactly what everyone's supposed to do, and then about three hours into the voyage the ship begins to sink, suddenly that's when you really find out who is going to do what and how it's going to work, who you can rely on and who you can't rely on in the middle of improvising something you have discovered something that you had never anticipated about the ship, etc., and that's very much like what it is to embark on any kind of large artistic project, especially obviously one that involves a lot of collaboration. People can approach it from completely different points of view, and I'd say it's no different for all practical purposes doing a piece of what might be called light entertainment in that way than it could be doing something that's considered very serious.

In attempting to illustrate the creative difficulties, both creative and logistic, that besiege film-making as a collaborative process, Thom highlights the simple but disarming fact that different film-makers working on the same project will often have very different views as to what kind of film they are making, let alone what kind of films they will actually be able to make. The latter point, the sinking ship analogy, again calls attention to the unpredictable nature of the process of film-making, its precarious status, where it is perfectly possible to have people on board that ship thinking they are working on one 'kind' of film where others think exactly the opposite. Any notion of an overall artistic 'signature' on a process of such complexity and unpredictability is a paradox by definition: both a necessity and a virtual impossibility. Without someone with a strong sense of where that ship may eventually need to go, once saved from sinking, the project would have no real hope of success. However, if sinking ships are anything to go by, it is difficult to hear what a captain may be shouting or directing you to do if all you are thinking about is how the hell to save your own life, professional or otherwise.

However, the differences between Murch and Thom's own positions in relation to authorship become evident when they discuss the role of personal creativity and its impact on the outcome of a film:

RT: I don't think the word 'create' describes very well the process of trying to do fresh work. Creating implies making something out of nothing. For me, the creative process is about reorganizing things that are already there ... The frame of mind in which interesting things germinate is often more confused and desperate than organized and confident.[12]

Thom believes less in creativity and art being the product of one's imagination where the latter means someone tapping into a very personal bag of creativity. He seems to indicate that in his view creativity emerges out of a process of discovery, or a trial and error process that is, to some important extent, independent of one's individual 'genius'. Unlike Thom, Murch seems to place greater emphasis on the importance of personal genius and of film-making as a means of personal expression for the director:

WM: That's been one of Francis's great strengths – finding ways to get his films to tap into his own personal experiences. I think sometimes that when films Francis has made have gone wrong, or not been as fully developed as they might have been, it's because he hasn't found a way to use his own life and experience as a reservoir from which to nourish those particular films. Then it tends to become a more technical exercise. But certainly in *The Godfather* films and *The Conversation* and *Apocalypse Now*, he was able to convert the making of those films into a kind of personal battleground and enrich the subject matter of the film itself.[13]

Final considerations

Murch and Thom's final thoughts shed some light on some very personal concerns about their role as film-makers and entertainers. They are words that struck a self-reflective note that we found was actually true of all professionals with whom we discussed these issues. Indeed, we were impressed by the seriousness with which everyone we interviewed responded to the questions we raised. In what is perhaps a revealing aspect, they all admitted to never really having been asked questions of this kind. We were left with a sense of omission that is hard to reconcile with notions of film-makers as simple clogs in an uncaring mechanism. There is more that deserves to be asked and debated.

RT: Isn't it funny that all of us are reluctant to admit that it's possible to simply entertain and not give anything else? I think it's, I don't know, maybe it's because I think that people just naturally seem to be about making up stories as a way of figuring out who they are in the world, and explaining things that go on around them. Any piece of entertainment, I think, will initiate that process in anybody that experiences that piece of entertainment, and different kinds of entertainment initiate in different ways, and obviously it's different for each person who receives it. But I am sceptical about whether anything, no matter how silly or superficial it might seem, is purely entertainment and no other benefit is derived from it. None of us certainly want to be thought of as simply an entertainer.

WM: One of the questions that keeps re-occurring on a daily basis to me is, what will people make of this? In the sense that I am giving them enough so that they can understand what's happening now. So I try to put myself as much as I can in the position of someone looking at the film for the first time. It's obviously not possible for me to do that, because I see the film thousands of times, but it is a skill that you have to develop to a certain extent. If you are completely oblivious to that, then I think you shouldn't be involved in this enterprise really. You have to think of the effect that it's going to have. Now the question is also, how do you then balance that with the internal requirements of the work itself, its organism? So, you have to think of the internal requirements of the organism and you have to think of the organism in its ecological environment which in film terms is the audience. The audience is the jungle in which this organism has to find its living and to find food, and to breathe, and to live, and to negotiate the difficulties, and to balance those two things. If you think only about what the audience is going to think, do they like this, do they like that, I think audiences like red so I'll put a lot of red in the film, and if they like red, then they'll do this, you ignore the internal requirements of the organism and you give to the audience something that is at best a bubble, a kind of thing that attracts the eye for a moment, but is kind of empty. On the other hand, if you think only about the organism of the film itself, with no reference to the ecology of the audience, then it may be a perfectly fine organism, but it has no environment to live in and it dies. So, it's a question of finding the right balance between those two things, and that right balance is always a guess.

Other views

In the interviews with Walter Murch and Randy Thom, we were able to explore at length film-makers' consciousness of themselves as entertainers. The issue is often touched on in interviews given by film-makers in other contexts. As a background to the interviews with Murch and Thom, we've provided some examples of the attitudes that are expressed.

Directors

Because of their position and because they are regularly interviewed, it's possible to get a good sense of directors' ideas. Jonathan Demme's (JD) views, which we discussed in our last book, was a starting point for this book:

> JD: I am very concerned with themes and psychological subtext in movies, but the thing that attracted me to *Married to the Mob* was the complete absence of themes and subtext, on one level. I liked the idea of trying to do a movie that was a complete escapist fantasy, which didn't pretend it had anything profound to say about anything. It was fun to do, and very cathartic, revivifying.
>
> AL: *Do you really mean it when you say* Married to the Mob *has nothing profound to say?*
>
> JD: Let's face it, *Married to the Mob* is a blatant attempt at a full tilt, crassly commercial entertainment – let's make no bones about that. Nevertheless, I did hope that if people liked the picture, part of their experience would be seeing this white person leave their comfortable, suburban, fully-equipped home and become an absolute outsider – Angela moves into profoundly more difficult living circumstances, surrounded by people who, through their ethnic definition or what have you, are relegated to a certain outsider status. Without beating it on the head, the audience sees: well, what do you know, down there people are people. When someone gives her a

chance at a job and sticks by her, because she's blessed with the absence of a racial distinction – she doesn't like people on the basis of what race they are – she's available to be reached out to. The fact that she's not a racialist proves to be an asset down there and helps her to get started on a new and positive path.

OK, that's probably corny, and it's not very well executed, but I feel it's as important an arena of thinking as exists in the world today. I mean, it's killing our society in a zillion ways, and it's so hard not to get sucked into the awfulness and the violence of racism, whether as an observer or a participant. Even when doing escapist movies like *Married to the Mob* you desperately want to try to get something positive, informationally, in there.[14]

The same kind of ambivalence is evident in Paul Greengrass's account of *The Bourne Trilogy*:

One of the things about the Bourne films I have always loved, although they are mainstream, commercial, Saturday-night popcorn movies, there's something about the story that enables you to get to the paranoia that drives the world today and express it in mainstream way.[15]

In his interviews, Spike Lee regularly touches on the relationship between entertainment and art:

If I was solely in the business of entertainment, I would not be making the movies I make. There would have been *She's Gotta Have It 2, 3, 4,* and *5.* I try to make entertainment that's also thought-provoking and has some intelligence behind it.[16]

Is your goal to make great art or to make massive entertainments?

I think that what I've done is always a combination of the two. For me, it's not a conflict. I don't want to make mindless entertainment, but at the same time I don't want to make shit no one understands either.[17]

Most of the movies that people are used to suck anyway! They're the same old tried and true formula, and at the end of the movie everything is wrapped up in a nice little bow. And very rarely do these movies make you think, and once you leave the theatre, by the time you're back on the subway or driving home, you've forgotten what you watched. It's like disposable entertainment. You sit there for two hours, and it washes over you and that's it … I think we don't demand enough of the audience. No subtlety, playing down to the lowest common denominator, making films for an intelligence level of retarded twelve-year-olds.[18]

Not surprisingly, Woody Allen is also a director who has views on the issues:

Art to me has always been entertainment for intellectuals. Mozart or Rembrandt or Shakespeare are entertainers on a very high level. It's a level that brings a great sense of excitement, stimulation and fulfilment to people who are sensitive and cultivated.[19]

[In] *Crimes and Misdemeanors* ... the murder is used for a moral discussion. Here, in the new film, it isn't [*Manhattan Murder Mystery*]. It's shallow and entertaining. Now I don't mean that to be critical of pure entertainment. That's fine. That has its place. Take Balanchine's *Nutcracker Suite*, for instance. That's light entertainment exclusively and there's a very important and significant place for this kind of thing. But I don't want to have any illusions about the movie ... I wanted it to be just light entertainment.[20]

David Cronenberg has been eloquent about the importance of art and its superiority over entertainment.

But it's my understanding of art as being subversive of civilization.[21]

I'm positing art as a means of coming to terms with death. Yes, I guess I'm putting art in opposition to religion, or as a replacement for religion, in the sense that if religion is used to allow you to come to terms with death and also to guide you in how to live your life, then I think art can do the same thing. But in a much less schematic way, in a much less rigid and absolute way, which is why it appeals to me and religion doesn't.[22]

An entertainer wants to give you exactly what you want. A good entertainer gives you those good old songs that you want to hear. And an artist wants to give you what you *don't know* you want. Something you might know you want the next time, but you never knew you wanted before.[23]

Otherwise, directors' views can easily be predicted from the kinds of films they make:

The Sergio Leone films were the ones that first allowed me to see there was more going on here than pure entertainment. Then I saw Fellini's *La Strada* and realized there was something here that didn't only aspire to poetry, that was poetry
(Neil Jordan)[24]

(Q) Do you enjoy deliberately frustrating people? (A) I look it as productive frustration. Films that are entertainments give simple answers but I think that's ultimately more cynical, as it denies the viewer room to think. If there are more answers at the end, then surely it is a richer experience.
(Michael Haneke)[25]

Art is useless. It has no utilitarian purpose. It is only an enrichment and then it becomes only a discovery or a surprise.
(Robert Altman)[26]

Producers

Producers are key figures in the film-making process but their ideas are more difficult to capture, since they are much less frequently interviewed than directors. The producers who do get interviewed tend to be of a certain kind so the range of views represented here is rather a narrow one.

Jerry Bruckheimer is the most uncompromising in his views.

> It's called *showbusiness*. And if you don't treat it as a business, you're in trouble. If you go into a very artistic endeavour, you have to do it for very little money. If you go into a big commercial endeavour – yes, you get a little more money. So you have to give a return on your money.
>
> (Jerry Bruckheimer)[27]

> Cinema has established itself as one of the most powerful and effective means we have, not just to entertain ourselves, but to express ourselves. ... Creative artists have a moral responsibility to challenge, inspire, question and affirm, as well as to entertain. Movies are more than fun and big business.
>
> (David Puttnam)[28]

> I think a lot of the movies I have done have entertained, but I think a lot of them also have something to say about the world in which we live, and I think that there's kind of an ethical obligation to enlighten and broaden the potential audience and the potential workforce.
>
> (David Picker)[29]

Writers

As might be anticipated, writers are often very articulate about the issues of art and entertainment. Their attitudes vary widely from Joe Esterhazy's full-on embrace of entertainment to Richard Price's savage disdain for it.

> If a movie does nothing more than entertain and amuse for an hour and a half, God bless it. There's enough misery out there, we don't need to add to it. Which is not to say that we shouldn't make films which are depressing also; there are some great depressing films. But it's too easy to slough off comedy as not being important and I think it's vitally important.
>
> (Phil Alden Robinson)[30]

> I write to entertain. I'm proud of doing that. I think one of the things that's been forgotten by writers today is their entertainment function. Dickens wrote to entertain – his books ran as serials in newspapers. It has somehow become low-rent to say that you're an entertainer. I know that I love sitting in a theater, sitting with the people watching one of my pictures when they're entertained or

when they're moved to silence or when they cry. It's one of the things I love most about what I do.

(Joe Esterhazy)[31]

I have, I suspect, come to want of it [art] more or less what Matthew Arnold wanted: that is, that it perform a function once the trust of religion, that of reconciling us to our experience, whether social, domestic, or tragic. I want an art that – through style, through wit, through vision, or through heart – redeems the experience it presents; the last thing I want is an art that idly documents discontents and as idly adds them to my own.

(Larry McMurtry)[32]

Not that you can't just tell wonderful entertainments, not that you can't tell good frightening and thrilling movies, but I think if you feel there's a higher purpose involved, your film is going to have a greater richness and a greater impact.

(Bruce Joel Rubin)[33]

I want to write what makes the most aesthetic sense, the most logical and emotional sense to me. You know, you create a real person, a very complex woman. Why bother to talk to all those shrinks and get a profile of how a woman would act like that if at the end Glenn Close is just going to turn into fucking Jason from the *Halloween* series?

(Richard Price)[34]

Actors

We've found few examples of actors' attitudes but Edward Norton's account of how he chose one of his roles is illuminating:

When I did *Primal Fear*, for example, I wasn't in the position of having a great deal of choice at that point in my career; having been offered it, I was obviously going to do it. But if I was to get a film like that right now, I would read it and say, 'This is a thriller – a piece of entertainment. That's my external assessment of it as a piece.' In the context of that piece, of course, my character, Aaron Stampler, is a completely amoral psychopath. But in terms of a story that has the goal of thrilling people, he's the key to the whole thing. And if you can scare people, that's a completely valid and worthwhile goal and one I have no problem with because I like thrillers, too. I like to get scared and I love the idea of giving people a great date movie to go and get scared at.[35]

Figure 6.1 *Singin' in the Rain*
(MGM/The Kobal Collection)

The first principle of Hollywood movie making is that a successful movie must
be entertaining. The theory is that people don't go to movies to be educated,
enlightened, or made better human beings, they go because they find it an
enjoyable experience ... The difficulty in applying this rule, however, is in
determining what is entertaining.[1]

6   The entertainment discourse

'Being entertaining should be of fundamental importance', declared a government White Paper on the future of the BBC. This provoked a *Guardian* journalist, Tim de Lisle, to ask 'What's entertainment?' He put the question to people who might be expected to know the answer. Their responses were vague which, on the face of it, is odd. The word is freely and confidently used in social and cultural analysis – it's often a key term in accounts of the character of the (post)modern world. Yet its meaning is elusive and not much elaborated upon.

Our own research produced similar results. We only found a few books and articles that discussed entertainment in any depth and they varied a good deal in quality. The most helpful were: two essays by Richard Dyer, 'The notion of entertainment' and 'Entertainment and Utopia'; a chapter in Richard Maltby's (2003) book *Hollywood Cinema*; and Shay Sayre and Cynthia King's *Entertainment & Society*.[2]

These accounts of entertainment differ in their aims and their scope. However, they agree on what they think the key features of entertainment are:

- Entertainment is a capitalist phenomenon. 'As a capitalist product, entertainment is developed to make money – there is always a bottom line to consider.'[3]
- The function of entertainment is to provide 'escape' for its audiences. 'Entertainment offers the image of "something better" to escape into, or something we want deeply that our day-to-day lives don't provide.'[4]
- Entertainment is easily accessible. 'Entertainment presents itself to us as wondrously benign. It offers us pleasure and makes no demands on us, except that it asks us not to think about it.'[5]

Both Dyer and Maltby focus their discussion of entertainment on Hollywood films. They both take the musical as the epitome of entertainment. Sayre and King's discussion has a much larger context that includes books, newspapers, magazines, television, popular music, radio, films, classical music, drama, opera, ballet, video games, gambling, sport and tourism.

The writers vary in their attitudes to entertainment. Dyer is the most positive. He argues that entertainment isn't an ersatz phenomenon but emerges from a recognition of real human needs. However, because of the demands of capitalist society, the response to those needs is a limited one. Maltby's position is close to Dyer's. However, his qualifications are so strong that the final effect is negative. He concludes his discussion by describing Hollywood entertainment as 'entirely solipsistic'. Sayre and King don't commit themselves to a judgement about entertainment as a whole: they simply describe what they think are its good and bad features.

Entertainment, industry and culture

Although there are few sustained attempts to answer the question, as we said, the word is frequently used both inside and outside academia as if its meaning was self-evident. What kind of account of entertainment emerges from an examination of these uses?

We identified two different contexts where the word has an important function. The first is economic and social, the second cultural. In the first context, entertainment has a limited and obvious use. It's used as a general label for a group of industries, which include television, radio, popular music, travel, sport and, increasingly, new developments such as video games and theme parks. These form the 'entertainment industry'. The products this industry offers are very different in kind, varying from films to tourist packages. The best way to see any unity between them is to understand entertainment as a synonym for leisure activities. Understood in this way, the use of entertainment in this context seems helpful. It captures many of the important things people look for in their leisure time – relaxation, amusement, distraction.

The use of entertainment in this way poses some problems, the main one being where the boundary lines for the group should be drawn. Many people spend their leisure time visiting art galleries and/or attending classical music concerts, yet art and classical music aren't usually identified as part of the entertainment industry. What principle excludes them? Isn't publishing also a part of the entertainment industry since many (though not all) of the books that come out are routinely identified as entertainment?

In the cultural context, entertainment is used for such wide and varied purposes that there appears to be nothing consistent or coherent behind its use. Sometimes it's used as if it referred to a general cultural phenomenon. Sometimes it's used to refer to a specific quality of films, television dramas, plays and novels. However, it is possible to recognize what we call an entertainment 'discourse'. Descriptions regularly highlight particular characteristics. This highlighting is usually accompanied by claims about the way entertainment functions.

Entertainment is light and limited

Whatever the use, a small number of adjectives and adverbs are commonly attached to entertainment: 'light', 'mere', 'pure', 'only', 'simply'.

> *New Jack City* was *pure* entertainment. It was not, quote, a serious film.[6]

> *Affliction* is not, by any stretch of even the most tortured imagination, *light* entertainment – or even conventional entertainment at all.[7]

> Yet this, in turn, has led to a kind of cultural flattening or standardisation where, in the place of debate and argument, there is *only* entertainment and art marketing.[8]

As these examples suggest, entertainment is characteristically identified in terms of its deficiencies and deleterious effects. It is perceived as lacking weight and substance, being unchallenging, offering only limited satisfactions to readers, viewers or listeners. A recurrent complaint about entertainment is that 'it doesn't make you think', 'As for entertainment cinema ... I suppose it can be alright ... when you prefer to think about nothing.'[9]

Because it is light and limited, entertainment is also believed to be unsuitable for the exploration of serious issues. A report on women's attitude to violence reported that *The Accused* (which deals with gang rape) 'had the most profound impact on the group' but that there was 'considerable concern about the appropriateness of a Hollywood film – one essentially premised on entertainment values – as the most suitable vehicle for dealing with this troubling subject'.[10]

Entertainment is consistently given a secondary and supporting role. So the film-maker Chris Petit 'expects the thriller to do its job: to intrigue and alarm, and also to deal with serious matters in the guise of entertainment'.[11] And the musician, Richard Thompson, echoes Petit almost exactly in his account of his music, 'It's like the blues, in the guise of entertainment you sing about problems.'[12]

The characterization of entertainment as a light and limited phenomenon has a powerful effect. We came across few expressions of positive attitudes towards it. If one was expressed, it was invariably accompanied by reservations '*It may not be great literature but it's great entertainment and far better written than much that pretends to higher things*'[13] (our italics). Most revealing are the defences offered by people who work in the entertainment industries. Joel Silver, the producer of blockbuster films like the *Die Hard* and *Lethal Weapon* series, offered this defence:

> I love these kind of movies. Why do you perceive *Lethal Weapon* as a lesser movie? Why is it lesser than something else – because it doesn't have a message? The message is entertainment, that's what our movies are about, entertainment. But they are also socially conscious films, they are multiethnic films, they are films with interesting roles for women, they always have interesting subtexts of different issues of the day.[14]

Silver begins with what seems to be an aggressive defence of entertainment in and for itself but then immediately concedes ground to his critics by suggesting that his films are not just entertainment but have another, socially conscious, dimension. In effect, he acknowledges the claim that entertainment lacks substance.

Entertainment is inferior to Art

Entertainment and art are regularly compared. The comparison is another powerful way of indicating entertainment's limitations because it's almost always made to demonstrate the superiority of art. The painter, Jake Chapman, expressed this position very clearly:

> If art is meant is meant to be simple, cultural entertainment, that's fine, we'll all just do sloppy paintings of anorexic nudes in baths. But art is not supposed to be easy. It is not an optical effect to make people feel good. It is not a happy drug.[15]

Art is seen as being demanding, critical, and having depth. It substantially engages with human experience and makes you think. Formally, it's complex and innovative; it's also personally expressive. In contrast, entertainment is undemanding, escapist and shallow. It accepts the world as it is and discourages thought. Its forms are simple and conservative; it's also impersonal and anonymous. This is to put the distinction in its strongest form. It's sometimes weakened – people will admit that art can be boring and self-important, that entertainment can be unpretentious and refreshing. But the basic value judgement is rarely disturbed.

We believe it should be disturbed because:

- Many works that are identified as art aren't, in an obvious sense, demanding – Jane Austen's novels, Mozart's operas, or Edward Hopper's paintings to give some obvious examples. Judging by their popularity with audiences, the pleasures gained from these are easily accessible.
- Many works that are identified as entertainment aren't, in an obvious sense, light distractions. Whatever their strengths and weaknesses, it's not accurate to describe a horror film like *The Exorcist*, a television drama like *24*, or a novel like *The Da Vinci Code* in this way.
- It is inaccurate to distinguish art from entertainment on the grounds that one is formally innovative and the other isn't. To take some contemporary examples, over the past 20 years the British and American novel hasn't been a particularly innovative area. Many highly regarded contemporary novels such as *On Beauty* or *Saturday* are formally traditional. Over the same time span, American television drama has been innovative. A crime drama like *Hill Street Blues* introduced multi-stranded, open-ended narratives. A comedy drama like *Northern Exposure* experimented with narrative pace and dramatic intensity. A legal drama like *Ally McBeal* undermined realism through its use of songs and fantasy.

The claim that entertainment isn't an area of personal expression is hard to sustain. A Jilly Cooper novel, a Linda LaPlante television drama, or a Burt Bacharach song are all easily recognizable in terms of their authors.

How difficult it is to maintain the distinction between entertainers and artists can be seen by the increasing frequency with which writers, film-makers, novelists, and musicians, whose work seem to have all the obvious characteristics of entertainment, are judged to be, in fact, artists. As we've already discussed, the classic example of this is Alfred Hitchcock. Once identified as an entertainer, he is now thought to be an artist. Where once his work was regarded as light and shallow, it is now celebrated as deep and profound. And the critical reputations of a number of other film-makers such as Howard Hawks, Samuel Fuller, Douglas Sirk and Frank Tashlin have changed in a similar way. Perhaps the most vivid symbol of this development was the analysis of Bob Dylan's song, 'Not dark yet', by the academic literary critic, Christopher Ricks. Ricks gave the lyric the same kind of attention and used the same critical tools as he would if he were analysing a poem by Philip Larkin or Seamus Heaney.

Art makes you think: entertainment doesn't

This claim really belongs in the previous section since it's one of the reasons given for the superiority of art over entertainment. We've isolated it because of its centrality.

Whenever the distinction is made, it's likely to be cited and its truth is taken for granted. The arguments and evidence that support this claim are, however, weak. Personal experience and anecdotal evidence suggest that, whether they are classed as entertainment or art, all kinds of novels, plays, TV dramas, paintings, or films can make you think. Indeed, there's almost no work that doesn't produce some thought, if it's only 'Why was that book/film/concert so bad? Why did I waste my time and money on it?' This flippant response reveals that the 'making you think' thesis isn't as straightforward as it appears. It isn't a demand for any kind of thought but for a certain quality of thought. But there are almost no demonstrations of if and how this quality of thought is achieved.

People who make this claim usually draw on ideas about alienation taken from the Russian Formalists and Bertolt Brecht in the first half of the twentieth century. But the concept of alienation only provides limited support. It demonstrates how novels, plays, poetry, films, etc. *may* put the audience into a *position* that encourages thought. Brecht's concept of epic theatre, for example, suggests that the nature of an epic play discourages an audience from close (emotional) identification with the story and the characters. By doing so, it opens up a space for the audience to reflect on what they've seen on the stage. Even if we accept that plays like *Mother Courage* or *Galileo* put their audiences into this position, Brecht still has to prove that his audiences did reflect and also provide evidence of the kind of reflection they made. So far as we know, there have been no serious attempts to provide this proof.

Entertainment encourages escapism

Entertainment is often criticized for the way it distracts people from serious issues:

> One of the functions of the concept of entertainment – by definition, that which we don't take seriously, or think about much ('It's only entertainment') – is to act as a kind of partial sleep of consciousness. For the filmmakers as well as the audience, full awareness stops at the level of plot, action and character, in which the most dangerous and subversive implications can disguise themselves and escape detection.[16]

The notion that entertainment encourages a 'sleep of consciousness' is often put more strongly by a comparison with drugs – 'With entertainment, moreover, as with drugs, the product eventually creates a demand for itself.'[17]

This belief has a long pedigree. The first version of it was directed at female readers of novels in the eighteenth century. John Brewer vividly describes prevailing attitudes:

> By the last years of the eighteenth century the female novel reader had become the epitome of the misguided reading public. She was depicted as filled with delusive ideas, swayed by false ideas of love and romance, unable to concentrate on serious matters – all of which would lead to frivolity, impulsiveness and possibly to sexual indiscretion.[18]

This linking of female readers, novels, and entertainment was, in fact, inaccurate. Brewer goes on to point out that, in fact, 'the flighty novel-reader was as likely to be male as female'. Despite its inaccuracy, the linking proved a long-lasting one. A hundred and fifty years later, Simone de Beauvoir, of all people, could write, 'In America ...writers are not popular, or if they are, it is only as entertainers. The women of the Pullman class, their primary readers, ask only to be amused.'[19]

The modern version of this belief supports an influential critique of Western society. It is used to explain the seeming political passivity of the mass of people and their unwillingness to confront the threats and injustices that characterize the modern world. One of the main reasons for this is entertainment's creation of idealized, fantastic and unreal worlds which distract audiences away from serious issues, usually conceived of in social/political terms as unemployment, war, the environment, and poverty.

We didn't find a strong justification for this belief. The characteristic justification took the form of analyses of novels, films or plays on the assumption that the qualities discovered in the analysis must have a direct effect on the reader/listener/viewer. This wasn't usually supported by investigations of reader/listener/viewer responses to establish if they were the anticipated ones. There are, however, two significant exceptions to this failure.

Janice Radway's (1991) *Reading the Romance* is a detailed and sensitive attempt to understand the responses of a group of women to romance novels of which they are enthusiastic readers. Radway's central question has a direct relevance to the 'entertainment as escape' thesis. The romances the women read centre on a male/female relationship where the typical ending of the story sees the hero win the heroine's affections by revealing that he has an emotional warmth and sensitivity. Radway acknowledges that the readers accept heterosexuality and marriage as a given and suggests that, from their viewpoint, reading the books is a mild protest against the restrictions of those practices. But she goes on to ask whether:

> [W]hen viewed from the vantage point of a feminism that would like to see the women's oppositional impulse lead to real social change, romance reading can also be seen as an activity that could potentially disarm that impulse. It might do so because it supplies vicariously those very needs and requirements that might otherwise be formulated as demands in the real world and lead to the potential restructuring of sexual relations.[20]

If romance novels do have this effect on their readers, Radway's research would provide strong support for the 'entertainment as escape' thesis. Her feminism in conjunction with her literary critical analysis of the romances clearly encourages her to believe that the books do act as an escape from real problems. However, her scholarly integrity prevents her from saying this is the case. She points out that her evidence doesn't allow her to conclude that the relationship between readers and romances works in this way. It would require much more knowledge of the women's family situations, their relations with their husbands, etc. before she could convincingly say it did. She also points out that the women themselves believe that reading the romances has a positive effect. For example, they regard some of the heroines they encounter in the books as 'namby-pamby' and believe that their response encourages them to behave differently in their own lives.

It is one of Janice Radway's strengths that she concludes *Reading the Romance* in an open-ended way. Certainly, her investigation gives some plausibility to the 'entertainment as escape' thesis. But it also makes other theses just as plausible. As we mentioned, reading romances may make readers better able to deal with the real world. Another conclusion that her evidence suggests is that reading romances has minimal effects which give no great cause for concern.[21]

The other relevant exploration of audience response is contained in *Bowling Alone*, Robert Putnam's well-known analysis of contemporary American society. In one section of the book, Putnam explores the relationship between civic engagement and television, 'Considered in combination with a score of other factors that predict social participation ... dependence on television for entertainment is not merely a significant predictor of civic disengagement. It is *the single most consistent* predictor that I have discovered.'[22]

This appears to offer well-founded support for the escapism thesis. However, the picture is more complicated. As Putnam admits, a correlation between a strong dependence on television entertainment and civic disengagement doesn't prove causation. It may be that civic disengagement leads to a dependence on television entertainment rather than the other way round. Putnam believes that television dependence is the cause rather than the consequence. The evidence he offers is, however, circumstantial and suggestive rather than direct and conclusive. But even if he is right, his evidence doesn't support a general 'entertainment is escape' thesis since Putnam identifies television entertainment as a special case. Entertainment provided by other media doesn't have the same consequences. The cinema provides a good example – 'Even within demographically matched groups, people who attend more movies also attend more club meetings, more dinner parties, more church services, and more public gatherings, give more blood, and visit with friends more often.'[23]

Putnam also cites evidence about the attitudes of heavy viewers of television entertainment which suggests that *they don't, in fact, find it all that entertaining.*

Art, pleasure and mass culture

It is helpful to place the contemporary discussion of entertainment in the context of two long-term debates. The first is a debate that has its roots in the eighteenth century when what we now identify as 'the arts' was separated from other human activities such as science and philosophy. This separation provoked a wide-ranging discussion about the distinctiveness of the arts. Early attempts to define this distinctiveness started from the observation that the arts aimed to give pleasure. Such a starting point inevitably provoked further questions. What kind of pleasure? How do we separate out the pleasure of art from the pleasure given by other human activities like food, sex, or games? This focus on pleasure also provoked anxiety about the value of the arts. If giving pleasure is what makes the arts distinctive, doesn't this suggest they are a frivolous activity, inferior to other activities like science or philosophy?

Although the focus has moved away from pleasure, the issue of what gives the arts their distinctiveness and value have remained central for aesthetics. An odd situation has developed. The belief that the arts are a distinctive and valuable human activity is widely held while a convincing justification for the belief continues to be elusive.[24] The philosopher, Charles Taylor, sums up the existing position very well when he writes:

> There is a kind of piety which still surrounds art and artists in our time, which comes from the sense that what they reveal has great moral and spiritual significance; that in it lies to the key to a certain depth, or fullness, or seriousness, or intensity of life, or to a certain wholeness. I have to use a string of alternatives here because this significance is very differently conceived, and often ... is not clearly conceived at all.[25] (For some examples that support Taylor's claim, see Appendix 4.)

The difficulty of justifying the value of art has led to the use of other strategies. One of the most favoured has been to make the case negatively. Art is compared with other things, whose inferiority seems obvious. At one time or another, these have included the novel, music hall, cinema, television, pop music, comics and video games. Over time, these have been grouped together as entertainment. The word is particularly apt for the comparison. Its dictionary definition, in this context, has a value judgement built into it. The New Oxford English dictionary definition of entertainment is 'the action of providing or being provided with amusement or enjoyment'. Amusement, of course, suggests comedy. In fact, Dr Johnson, in his dictionary, claimed the word entertainment applied specifically to 'lower comedy'. And the dictionary gives as examples of entertainers, 'singers, dancers or comedians'. The overall effect the definition creates is of an engaging experience but one that isn't deep and/or intense and/or serious. The value of art is highlighted by entertainment's limitations – entertainment is light, art is substantial.

The debate provoked by the emergence of mass culture also illuminates the concept of entertainment. It's a debate that has close connections with the one about art. Both have a similar ancestry in the late eighteenth and early nineteenth centuries when a rapidly growing middle class with time and money to devote to leisure made the novel a popular form. This was one of the first and most obvious signs of the emergence of 'mass culture'. The novel was one of the first signs of change. New forms like photography, film, radio and television followed. New ways of manufacturing and distributing those forms were developed. The composition of the audience changed: the middle class and the working class came together to constitute a mass audience.

For those who thought of themselves as being involved in the 'fine arts' – poets, dramatists, painters, composers, critics and theorists – these developments appeared to be a threat. At the beginning of this era, William Wordsworth wrote:

> For a multitude of causes, unknown to former times, are now acting with a combined force to blunt the discriminating powers of the mind, and unfitting it for all voluntary exertion to reduce it to a state of almost savage torpor. The most effective of these causes are the great national events which are daily taking place [such as the war with France], and the increasing accumulation of men in cities produces a craving for extraordinary incident which the rapid communication of intelligence hourly gratifies. To this tendency of life and manners the

literature and theatrical exhibitions of the country have conformed themselves. The invaluable works of our elder writers, I had almost said the works of Shakespeare and Milton, are driven into neglect by frantic novels, sickly and stupid German tragedies, and deluges of idle and extravagant stories in verse.[26]

The art/entertainment distinction is already implicit in Wordsworth's comments.

Does entertainment exist?

So, to return to our original question, what is entertainment? The question depends on the assumption that entertainment is a distinct phenomenon with a clear identity. Most people who discuss entertainment take this for granted. But the few people who have seriously tried to say what entertainment is demonstrate how elusive a phenomenon it is. Richard Dyer, one of the most thoughtful writers on the topic, claims:

> Entertainment is a type of performance produced for profit, performed before a generalised audience (the 'public'), by a trained, paid group who do nothing else but produce performances which have the sole (conscious) aim of providing pleasure.[27]

This description confines entertainment to performance arts like theatre, film and television, ignoring non-performance ones like novels and comics. It excludes amateur work. A rock group performing in a local pub or a theatre group in a church hall are normally regarded as offering entertainment, even though the performers may not be paid or trained. And if production for profit is a criterion, then nothing that the BBC produces can be regarded as entertainment.

Far from being distinctive with a well-defined identity, we'd describe entertainment as an amorphous phenomenon, whose amorphousness allows it to be used in a variety of contexts: social and economic (the entertainment industries), aesthetic (entertainment opposed to art) and critical (the entertainment dimension of a work). From our examination of its uses, the only overall sense we could discern was that entertainment was a synonym for mass culture. Whenever entertainment is discussed, examples of mass culture are cited: soap operas, pop songs, action movies, crime novels, reality television programmes. And when the entertainment industry is characterized, it's the mass culture forms, like cinema, television, and popular music that are foregrounded. It's also revealing that while 'mass entertainment' is a common expression, 'minority entertainment' isn't. The masses have entertainment and the minority has art.

When entertainment becomes a synonym for mass culture, a covert operation is performed. From the late 1940s on, the distinction between mass and minority culture – central to cultural debate in the first half of the twentieth century – has been weakened both by critics and artists. The way entertainment is conceived resurrects the distinction in a strong form. The same accusations are directed at entertainment that used to be directed at mass culture: it's insubstantial, escapist, and commercial; it's not innovative; it's uncritical; and it's socially and politically conservative. On the basis of this account, entertainment (along with consumerism) has become a central term in a frequently made critique of contemporary *mass* society.

It's a critique we're unsympathetic to because entertainment becomes one of the props of a simplistic, anti-capitalist position, especially in relation to Hollywood. Susan Sontag's all-out attack on modern cinema provides an example whose extravagance highlights the weaknesses of this critique:

> This doesn't mean that there won't be any more new films that one can admire. But such films won't simply be exceptions; that's true of great achievement in any art. They have to be heroic violations of the norms and practices which now govern movie-making everywhere in the capitalist and would-be capitalist world – which is to say, everywhere. And ordinary films, *films made purely for entertainment [that is, commercial] purposes*, will continue to be astonishingly witless; already the vast majority fail resoundingly to reach their cynically targeted audiences.[28]

Sontag offers a horror comic version of capitalism. For her, it's a monolithic and all-pervasive form – the capitalists have either got you or they're coming to get you! She connects entertainment with capitalism by making it an interchangeable term with 'commercial', a word which implies the dominance of the profit motive. In this way she establishes an equation: capitalism = commercial = entertainment.

Entertainment is marked as a capitalist phenomenon which allows Sontag to describe ordinary (entertainment) films as witless, cynically targeted products that, she claims, audiences don't respond to. Apart from the cartoon version of capitalism, the biggest objection to attacks like this is that they never offer an alternative to capitalist methods of cultural production. To do so, it would be necessary to confront the complex challenges posed by the relative success of democratic capitalist societies as against the decay and collapse of the socialist societies in the second half of the twentieth century.

A lack of interest in or an antipathy towards mass tastes also weakens the critique politically. Audiences are too easily characterized as passive/uncritical/undemanding/easily distracted. Sontag's attack certainly displays a lack of interest in audience reaction – a capitalist industry would go out of business if the majority of its products 'failed resoundingly'. Her claim is, in fact, inaccurate, as some research would have shown her. Audiences for Hollywood films during the last quarter of the twentieth century were remarkably buoyant. This is hardly evidence of audience dissatisfaction.[29]

Final thoughts

1. Entertainment shouldn't be reified. It isn't a well-defined, substantial phenomenon. The word generally functions as shorthand for a characterization of mass culture as insubstantial and lightweight. At various points in this book, especially in Chapter 1, we demonstrated how limited and approximate that characterization is. We believe the way it's used is particularly unfortunate because it creates either a suspicion of pleasure or suggests it's a secondary experience, no more than the icing on the cake.
2. Art should be dethroned from the status that is claimed for it. It doesn't have an

inherent value. There's good art and bad art. Art should be a descriptive term not a value one, which encompasses all the activities associated with making and watching films, writing and reading novels, composing and listening to music, or painting and looking at pictures.

3. Consequently, the entertainment/art distinction should be abandoned. Everything should be treated as art. Meaningful distinctions could then be made between different kinds of art, based on creative traditions, audiences, and economic structures.

4. Any proper account of audience responses should value light and ephemeral experiences as well as 'heavy' and long-lasting ones. The pleasures of watching films (or reading novels or listening to music) are many and varied. Similarly, the desire for distraction or escape doesn't deserve an immediate red card! The concept of a person who is always fully engaged with and attentive to the central issues of their time is rather forbidding, with its strong puritanical emphasis.

One of our biggest hopes in writing this book is that it would encourage a more serious interest in audience pleasures (and displeasures!). We join with Mr Sleary, the lisping circus-owner in Charles Dickens' *Hard Times*, when he admonishes Mr Gradgrind: 'People must be amuthed, Thquire, thomehow ... Make the beth of uth; not the wortht.'

Appendix 1
Methodology for statistical analysis

This appendix explains the various parameters and choices pertaining to Chapter 1. We hope it will facilitate the use and understanding of that chapter. Should you have any further queries concerning the database or its content and analysis please refer to the tables in Chapter 1. We have tried there to explain more about the reasons for our choices in relation to the themes and subject matter of this book. However, should you have any further queries, please feel free to email us at: gianluca.sergi@nottingham.ac.uk

1 Selection of material

We gathered data from a variety of sources (see below for further details) pertaining to two main groups. The first, which we called Mass Audience List (MAL hereon) refers to films that have enjoyed success on a mass scale with audiences in the USA. The second group, which we called Elite Audience List (EAL hereon) contains films that have attracted particular praise from critics and scholars. The terms Mass and Elite were not meant as suggestive of quality but rather as mirroring traditional definition of the two respective audiences: mass entertainment the former, elitist art the latter.

Mass Audience List

The films in this list come from the top 50 box-office grossing films of all time on the US market as of 1 September 2007. All figures were adjusted for inflation and take into account multiple releases of films. The data was crosschecked from at least three sources. The primary site for information was the professional version of Box Office Mojo (note: pay subscription is required for the professional version of the site). We chose this above other sites as they provided stronger data on figure adjustment and allow users to adjust figures both in terms of year of release and tickets sold. This allows researchers to use tickets sold multiplied by average ticket price multiplied by potential multi-release patterns as a means of reaching an estimated figure adjusted for inflation rather than using the conventional 'shortcut' of adjusting directly the box office result of a film taking into account actual inflation. The latter method does not allow for difference in ticket price, number of tickets sold or multiple releases of a film. Given the time, we would have liked to fine tune this further by looking at increases in population, patterns of release and other similar data. However, given the number of films involved, that kind of detailed statistical analysis would require a much larger project.

Despite the strength and validity of the data, we chose to cross-reference it by utilizing other similar up-to-date research tools. In particular, we found the following useful: (1) *The Movie Times*; (2) *The Numbers*; and (3) *Box Office Guru*.[1]

This is the list of films we researched for the Mass Audience list. They are in the top 50 grossing films adjusted for inflation on 1 September 2007.[2]

1 *Gone With the Wind*   1939   V. Fleming
2 *Star Wars*   1977   G. Lucas
3 *The Sound of Music*   1965   R. Wise
4 *E.T.*   1982   S. Spielberg
5 *The Ten Commandments*   1956   C. B. DeMille
6 *Titanic*   1997   J. Cameron
7 *Jaws*   1975   S. Spielberg
8 *Doctor Zhivago*   1965   D. Lean
9 *The Jungle Book*   1967   W. Reitherman
10 *Snow White and the Seven Dwarfs*   1937   D. Hand
11 *Ben-Hur*   1959   W. Wyler
12 *One Hundred and One Dalmatians*   1961   C. Geronimi/H. Luske
13 *The Exorcist*   1973   W. Friedkin
14 *The Empire Strikes Back*   1980   I. Kershner
15 *Return of the Jedi*   1983   R. Marquand
16. *The Sting*   1973   G. Roy Hill
17. *Mary Poppins*   1964   R. Stevenson
18 *Raiders of the Lost Ark*   1981   S. Spielberg
19 *Jurassic Park*   1993   S. Spielberg
20 *Star Wars – Episode I – The Phantom Menace*   1999   G. Lucas
21. *The Graduate*   1967   M. Nichols
22. *Fantasia*   1940   J. Algar/S. Armstrong
23 *The Godfather*   1972   F. Ford Coppola
24 *Forrest Gump*   1994   R. Zemeckis
25 *Close Encounters of the Third Kind*   1977   S. Spielberg
26. *The Lion King*   1994   R. Allers/R. Minkoff
27. *Sleeping Beauty*   1959   M. Banta/W. Hibler
28. *Grease*   1978   R. Kleise
29. *Shrek 2*   2004   A. Adamson/K. Asbury
30. *Butch Cassidy and the Sundance Kid*   1969   G. Roy Hill
31. *Bambi*   1942   J. Algar/S. Armstrong
32 *Spider-Man*   2002   S. Raimi
33 *Independence Day*   1996   R. Emmerich
34. *Love Story*   1970   A. Hiller
35. *Beverly Hills Cop*   1984   M. Brest
36. *Pinocchio*   1940   H. Luske/B. Sharpsteen
37. *Home Alone*   1990   C. Columbus
38 *Cleopatra*   1963   J. L. Mankiewicz
39 *Airport*   1970   G. Seaton
40. *American Graffiti*   1973   G. Lucas
41 *Ghostbusters*   1984   I. Reitman

42 *The Robe*   1953   H. Koster
43 *Pirates of the Caribbean – Dead Man's Chest*   2006   G. Verbinski
44. *Around the World in 80 Days*   1956   M. Anderson
45 *LOTR – The Return of the King*   2003   P. Jackson
46. *Blazing Saddles*   1974   M. Brooks
47 *Batman*   1989   T. Burton
48. *The Bells of St. Mary's*   1945   L. McCarey
49 *The Towering Inferno*   1974   I. Allen/J. Guillermin
50 *Spider-Man 2*   2004   S. Raimi

Elite Audience List

The films chosen from this list are the top 50 films as indicated in the longest running poll of critics/scholars and directors, the BFI/Sight and Sound Top 10 Best Films. The poll has been published ten-yearly since 1952, our selection is from the latest version, published in 2002. Although the poll highlights the top 10 films, the fuller list is available, making possible to view the top 100 films.[3]

The films in the EAL are:[4]

1 *Citizen Kane*   1941   Orson Welles
2 *Vertigo*   1958   Alfred Hitchcock
3 *La Règle du jeu*   1939   Jean Renoir
4 *The Godfather I & II*   1972   Francis F. Coppola
5 *Tokyo Story*   1953   Yasujiro Ozu
6 *2001 – A Space Odyssey*   1968   Stanley Kubrick
7 *Battleship Potemkin*   1925   Sergei Eisenstein
8 *Sunrise*   1927   Friedrich W. Murnau
9 *8½*   1963   Federico Fellini
10 *Singin' in the Rain*   1952   Gene Kelly and Stanley Donen
11 *Seven Samurai*   1954   Akira Kurosawa
12 *The Searchers*   1956   John Ford
13 *Rashomon*   1950   Akira Kurosawa
14 *The Passion of Joan of Arc*   1928   Carl Theodor Dreyer
15 *A bout de souffle*   1961   Jean-Luc Godard
16 *L'Atalante*   1934   Jean Vigo
17 *The General*   1927   Buster Keaton
18 *Touch of Evil*   1958   Orson Welles
19 *Au hasard Balthazar*   1966   Robert Bresson
20 *Jules et Jim*   1962   François Truffaut
21 *L'avventura*   1961   Michelangelo Antonioni
22 *Le Mépris*   1963   Jean-Luc Godard
23 *Pather Panchali*   1955   Satyajit Ray
24 *La dolce vita*   1961   Federico Fellini
25 *M*   1931   Fritz Lang
26 *The Story of the Late Chrysanthemums*   1939   Mizoguchi
27 *Barry Lyndon*   1975   Stanley Kubrick

28 *Les Enfants du paradis*   1946   Michel Carné
29 *Ivan the Terrible*   1944   Sergei M. Eisenstein
30 *Man with a Movie Camera*   1929   Dziga Vertov
31 *Metropolis*   1927   Fritz Lang
32 *Some Like It Hot*   1959   Billy Wilder
33 *Ugetsu Monogatari*   1954   Kenji Mizoguchi
34 *Wild Strawberries*   1957   Ingmar Bergman
35 *Andrei Roublev*   1969   Andrei Tarkovsky
36 *The 400 Blows*   1959   François Truffaut
37 *Fanny and Alexander*   1983   Ingmar Bergman
38 *La Grande Illusion*   1937   Jean Renoir
39 *The Magnificent Ambersons*   1942   Orson Welles
40 *Modern Times*   1936   Charles Chaplin
41 *Psycho*   1960   Alfred Hitchcock
42 *The Seventh Seal*   1958   Ingmar Bergman
43 *Taxi Driver*   1976   Martin Scorsese
44 *The Third Man*   1949   Carol Reed
45 *Bicycle Thieves*   1948   Vittorio De Sica
46 *Blade Runner*   1982   Ridley Scott
47 *City Lights*   1931   Charles Chaplin
48 *Greed*   1924   Eric von Stroheim
49 *Intolerance*   1916   D. W. Griffith
50 *Lawrence of Arabia*   1963   David Lean

2 Organization of material

The database we created was divided into two main tables. One dealt with the MAL data, the other with the EAL data. Ultimately, over 20 variables were introduced in the database to allow us to interrogate the data from each film and aggregate it according to specific parameters (please see details below). Finally, we compared the data whenever the questions we were asking of it required us to do so.

The following is a full list of the variables we considered in relation to the data for the films in both lists. They are presented in no particular order. Some of the variables (for instance, year of release, ratings, box office, etc.) do not require any particular explanation. In all other cases we include a brief explanation of the option we included when interrogating the data. Finally, there are several cases when it was necessary to include value lists (i.e. several possible answers to any one question). In these cases we have included a lengthier explanation of both the composition of those value lists and their significance.

List of variables

- *Rating*: the rating of a film.
- *Genre(s)*: the genre(s) of a film. Although we tried to be as precise as possible (mostly by limiting the number of genres to the most significant to the story),

the nature of this variable is such that inevitably most films were listed under more than one genre. For instance, *Forrest Gump* utilizes several generic conventions that belong to Drama, Comedy and Romance, and is categorized accordingly. We later noticed some interesting results when grouping films along three key headings/organizing principles that we defined as follows: (1) Unreal genres: sci-fi, fantasy and animation; (2) Light-hearted genres: comedy, romance, musical; and (3) Serious genres: crime, drama, biography. The terms we employed to group these genres refer to popular notions of those respective genres. There are of course musicals that could be described as either unreal or not entirely light-hearted. Similarly, there are different ways to approach the subject matter in any given genre, ranging from the light-hearted to the downbeat. However, the data clearly showed the prevalence of certain combinations of films, and that those combinations broadly followed the lines in which audiences tend to refer to and think of the genres involved.

- *Director*: the director(s) of a film.
- *Adjusted BO*: Adjusted Box-Office according to inflation (see p. 104 for information on inflation adjustment).
- *Source*: is the film based on an original screenplay or is it adapted from an existing source?
- *Situation*: what kind of situation does the story present for its characters? The values used here were: (1) Ordinary; (2) Extraordinary; (3) Fantastic/Supernatural; and (4) Other. The choice of one of these values depended on the situation in which the main character operates, not on the nature and abilities of the character him/herself. For instance, an ordinary man placed under extreme circumstances would produce a result of Extraordinary. An extraordinary character placed in an ordinary everyday context may result in an Ordinary value. The value of 'Other' was added to include mostly animated films, which often escape traditional definitions of 'reality', hence transcending somewhat notions of the ordinary. Examples for each category are: *Tokyo Story* (ordinary), *The Towering Inferno* (extraordinary), *Jurassic Park* (fantastic/supernatural), and *Shrek 2* (other).
- *Timeframe*: when is the film set in relation to present time? The values used here were: (1) Present; (2) Past; (3) Future; (4) Unspecified. The latter category mostly concerns films that are set in no specific time or in a timeless setting. Examples of this category are films such as *Lord of the Rings – The Return of the King* and most animated films.
- *Location*: where is the film set in geographical terms? To avoid including too many variables we chose to group the data according to the following variables: (1) US – Urban setting; (2) International – Urban setting; (3) US – Other; (4) International – Other; (5) Unspecified. The last category refers mostly to films that are virtually impossible to attribute to an urban or other setting (i.e. countryside, mountains, seaside, etc.), choose specifically to avoid identification of locale, or where the plot continually moves from one type of location to another. For instance, *Star Wars* and other sci-fi films are often located in space or some undefined urban settlement and are thus difficult to be identified as belonging to a specific setting in a conclusive manner. Similarly, animated films

are often set in magical kingdoms or spaces that do not necessarily fall under any conventional category, such as in *Shrek 2* and *Sleeping Beauty*.

- *Status*: how important is the financial status of a character to the development of the story? We had six values in this complex list:
wealthy, comfortable, struggling, poor, rich–poor relationship, insignificant to story. The first four categories are relatively self-explanatory, though obviously not altogether unproblematic. The latter two, however, required us to think carefully about their meaning to the survey and deserve further explanation. Where we felt that the relationship between the main characters or the plot itself revolved around directly set up contrasting positions based on wealth (for instance, in *Beverly Hills Cop* the character played by Eddie Murphy, detective Axel Foley, is a financially struggling policeman who ends up pursuing rich bad guys with seemingly unlimited resources), we used the rich–poor relationship option. Conversely, if we felt that the financial status of the characters did not truly come into play in the film narrative (as in the case of *Grease*, for instance) we chose to use the insignificant to story option.
- *Ticket price*: this is the average ticket price for the year of release of the film. We mostly used this variable to crosscheck for consistencies when addressing issue of economic performance of a film against the overall landscape of film production and cost of admission.
- *Ending*: is the ending of a film happy, unhappy, other? We chose four options: (1) Happy ending; (2) Unhappy ending; (3) Ambiguous ending; and (4) Open ending. We are obviously aware of the interpretative nature of most of these options (what may seem a happy ending for some may ring as rather more ambiguous to others as to whether it is happy or unhappy, or even seem downright unhappy). The principle we chose to apply is that of degree of ambiguity. If there is no real sense of doubt as to the ending of a film is happy, unhappy or open, then we chose one of those three options. Wherever we felt there was a considerable degree of interpretation left open by the ending, we chose the ambiguous ending option.
- *Star*: the star status of key actors in the film. We chose to have four possible options: (1) marquee; (2) recognizable; (3) none; (4) inapplicable (animation). The latter option caused a certain amount of unease as we wanted to recognize the fact that films like *Shrek* featured the voices of a marquee star such as Mike Myers and other very recognizable actors such as Eddie Murphy and Cameron Diaz. However, in the end, we decided to adhere to a more traditional view of 'actors' as real actors as opposed to voice acting alone. We wish to stress that this is not to suggest that the visual aspects of acting are more important or relevant than the vocal aspects. We simply agreed that it made more sense for the specific purpose of this study to retain the traditional notion of actor.

In all cases we referred our selection in relation to US audiences rather than the country of origin of the film. This is obviously particularly important in relation to the foreign language database. For instance, while Gerard Dépardieu was one of the most bankable stars on the French market at the time of the release of *Cyrano de Bergerac*, he was, at best, a recognizable figure for US audiences.

- *Best Picture*: the category considered here are two: for the MAL we looked at which of the films in the list had been awarded the Best Picture Oscar for the year in which they were released. As the vast majority of films in the EAL were non-US films, we chose also to consider whether films in the EAL had been awarded either the Best Picture Oscar or the Best Foreign Picture Oscar.

- *Epic*: does the film aim for epic stature? The notion of the 'epic' is here understood in a multifaceted fashion. A film may present a story which calls for a character to perform epic feats (*Ben Hur*); also, a film may be epic in scale (*Gone With the Wind*); a film may also be about an epic figure (*Cleopatra*, *The Ten Commandments*) or it may place the main characters at the centre of an epic struggle (war, famine, etc.).

- *Individual*: how relevant is the presence of a known director/producer to the success of a film? We chose here not to consider stars since we had a different value for them. Besides stars, two figures have had an impact historically on the success, critical and/or popular, of a film, producers and, increasingly since the late 1950s, directors.

- *Black and White*: does the film use black and white cinematography? We wanted to avoid assuming that audiences of either lists necessarily preferred colour over black and white and we decided to include this variable to the database.

- *Life and Death*: does the film present the main characters with a life-and-death situation? As we were beginning to get a sense of the kind of results the database was yielding we noticed a trend in both lists to place characters in a situation where failure does not 'merely' result in losing a job or a failed marriage but in death. We thus chose to test it fully by including this variable.

- *Family*: is film 'x' primarily addressed to family audiences? One of the main assumptions about Mass Audiences and popular entertainment is that in choosing to see films that are broadly speaking aimed at a family audience they have unwittingly caused a move away from adult stories and treatment of stories. We decided to test this assumption, hence the inclusion of this variable. We appreciate that it is extremely difficult to be categorical about this variable: some films obviously appeal to both family audiences and adult audiences. For the purpose of this study, we chose to elect films that had family audiences as their primary intended target as 'Family' films.

- *Gender*: this variable measures the instances of the presence of a female character who is central to a film's narrative and its development. It does not measure the number of films that have significant female roles in them. Rather it attempts to gauge the frequency of women being given a 'primary' active role in a film, where her actions effect change or determine story outcome in ways that are not simply incidental or accidental.

- *Race*: similar to Gender, this variable aims to provide an indication of the frequency of a black character who is central to the narrative and its development.

- *Technology*: films whose success may, in part at least, be ascribed to the extensive use and showcasing of technology. There are obviously degrees to which this variable can be attributed to various films, but there are clear differences between films such as *Jurassic Park* and *Independence Day*, where the technology is directly on display and very much part of the attraction, and films such as *Raiders of the*

Lost Ark and *Doctor Zhivago* where the extensive use of sophisticated technologies in production is actually presented to audiences in ways other than a technological spectacle (*Raiders* by suggesting the return to old-fashioned adventure B-movies and *Zhivago* by invoking prestige and literary adaptation as their main *raison d'être*).

- *Entertainment*: films that are primarily attempting at entertaining audiences. Following on from the previous variable, we decided to ask a simple, though deceptive question: how many of the films in either list can be unequivocally classified as 'exercises in entertainment'? Again, as with technology before, it is extremely difficult to be categorical. However, films like *The Godfather*, *The Exorcist* and *Lord of the Rings – The Return of the King*, while clearly being entertaining clearly show a definite ambition to do more than provide basic entertainment, be this in terms of their scope, subject matter, treatment of topic, adult material. Conversely, films such as *Airport, Raiders of the Lost Ark* and *Pirates of the Caribbean – Dead Man's Chest* do not, on the surface at least, suggest an intention to discuss any wider issues other than those immediately facing their main characters. We would like to stress that this variable is not designed as an issue of quality or value but rather as an attempt to measure the presence of direct entertainment in both lists.

3 Data crunching and interpretation

We fed all data and variables into a large database using Filemaker Pro 9 as the chosen software. This allowed us to search fully the data creating as many permutations and combinations as we thought useful. In order to ensure that we covered as many relevant issues and variables as possible, we also looked for inspiration to secondary sources, such as interviews with film-makers, film reviews, and viewers' comments. The final results and their interpretation, however, were entirely based on data.

We also created a similar database for the top 50 Foreign Language Box Office hits in the USA, again adjusted for inflation. We used this data mostly for two key reasons. First, we wanted to check that the variables we were using applied beyond the framework of reference that we had set: if we were to suggest possible ways to do quantitative analysis of films, the issue of method and its validity was obviously very important. Second, we wished to have the option of cross-referencing unusual results to ensure that the questions asked and the variables applied did not artificially skew the results. Obviously there is always a human element of bias in the design of databases, the gathering of data and its interpretation, so we hoped this third list would help us iron out any particular deficiency in our approach. The Foreign List data do not figure in this study, mostly for logistical reasons, but also because, unlike the MAL and EAL, the data pertaining to Foreign Language films are more sketchy and it is more difficult to triangulate information from different sources given the paucity of the latter.

Appendix 2
Walter Murch's filmography

Theatrical releases only – as of September 2008.

As film editor

- *Youth Without Youth* (2007)
- *Jarhead* (2005)
- *Dickson Experimental Sound Film (1894)* (2003 release)
- *Cold Mountain* (2003)
- *K-19: The Widowmaker* (2002)
- *The Talented Mr. Ripley* (1999)
- *Dumbarton Bridge* (1999)
- *Touch of Evil* (1958) (1998 version)
- *The English Patient* (1996)
- *First Knight* (1995)
- *I Love Trouble* (1994)
- *Romeo Is Bleeding* (1993)
- *House of Cards* (1993)
- *The Godfather Trilogy: 1901–1980* (1992) (V)
- *The Godfather: Part III* (1990)
- *Ghost* (1990)
- *Call from Space* (1989)
- *The Unbearable Lightness of Being* (1988)
- *Captain EO* (1986)
- *Apocalypse Now* (1979)
- *Julia* (1977)
- *The Conversation* (1974)
- *The Godfather* (1972)

As sound designer/editor

- *Youth Without Youth* (2007)
- *Jarhead* (2005)
- *Cold Mountain* (2003)
- *K-19: The Widowmaker* (2002)
- *The Talented Mr. Ripley* (1999)

- *The English Patient* (1996)
- *First Knight* (1995)
- *Crumb* (1994)
- *Romeo Is Bleeding* (1993)
- *The Godfather: Part III* (1990)
- *Ghost* (1990)
- *Dragonslayer* (1981)
- *Apocalypse Now* (1979)
- *The Godfather: Part II* (1974)
- *The Conversation* (1974)
- *American Graffiti* (1973)
- *THX 1138* (1971)
- *Gimme Shelter* (1970)
- *The Great Walled City of Xan* (1970)
- *The Rain People* (1969)

As writer and/or director

- *Return to Oz* (1985)
- *The Black Stallion* (1979)
- *THX 1138* (1971)

Appendix 3
Randy Thom's filmography

Theatrical releases only – as of September 2008.

As sound designer/mixer/editor

- *Horton Hears a Who!* (2008)
- *Standard Operating Procedure* (2008)
- *Beowulf* (2007)
- *Enchanted* (2007)
- *The Simpsons Movie* (2007)
- *Ratatouille* (2007)
- *Eragon* (2006)
- *Monster House* (2006)
- *Zidane, un portrait du 21e siècle* (2006)
- *Over the Hedge* (2006)
- *Ice Age: The Meltdown* (2006)
- *Harry Potter and the Goblet of Fire* (2005)
- *War of the Worlds* (2005)
- *The Incredibles* (2004)
- *The Polar Express* (2004)
- *Shrek 2* (2004)
- *Inosensu: Kôkaku kidôtai* (2004)
- *Lara Croft Tomb Raider: The Cradle of Life* (2003)
- *Shrek 4-D* (2003)
- *Darkness Falls* (2003)
- *Harry Potter and the Chamber of Secrets* (2002)
- *Windtalkers* (2002)
- *Osmosis Jones* (2001)
- *Final Fantasy: The Spirits Within* (2001)
- *Avalon* (2001)
- *Cast Away* (2000)
- *What Lies Beneath* (2000)
- *Reindeer Games* (2000)
- *Bicentennial Man* (1999)
- *Snow Falling on Cedars* (1999)
- *In Too Deep* (1999)

- *The Iron Giant* (1999)
- *Arlington Road* (1999)
- *Forces of Nature* (1999)
- *Stepmom* (1998)
- *Plug* (1998)
- *Starship Troopers* (1997)
- *Mimic* (1997)
- *Contact* (1997)
- *Mars Attacks!* (1996)
- *Chain Reaction* (1996)
- *The Frighteners* (1996)
- *Jumanji* (1995)
- *Nine Months* (1995)
- *Species* (1995)
- *Disclosure* (1994)
- *Miracle on 34th Street* (1994)
- *Forrest Gump* (1994)
- *Yellowstone* (1994)
- *The Nutcracker* (1993)
- *The Saint of Fort Washington* (1993)
- *Siu nin Wong Fei Hung ji: Tit Ma Lau* (1993) *(US version)*
- *House of Cards* (1993)
- *Homeward Bound: The Incredible Journey* (1993)
- *A Brief History of Time* (1991)
- *Backdraft* (1991)
- *The Dark Wind* (1991)
- *Wild at Heart* (1990)
- *Cry-Baby* (1990)
- *Cold Dog Soup* (1990)
- *Always* (1989)
- *The Thin Blue Line* (1988)
- *Tucker: The Man and His Dream* (1988)
- *Colors* (1988)
- *The Couch Trip* (1988)
- *Spaceballs* (1987)
- *Gardens of Stone* (1987)
- *Howard the Duck* (1986)
- *Ewoks: The Battle for Endor* (1985) (TV)
- *The Mean Season* (1985)
- *Latino* (1985)
- *Grand Canyon: The Hidden Secrets* (1984)
- *Star Trek III: The Search for Spock* (1984)
- *Indiana Jones and the Temple of Doom* (1984)
- *The Right Stuff* (1983)
- *Rumble Fish* (1983)
- *Never Cry Wolf* (1983)

- *Return of the Jedi* (1983)
- *Koyaanisqatsi* (1982)
- *The Empire Strikes Back* (1980)
- *Apocalypse Now* (1979)

Appendix 4
Art

Art is an irritant; its silent insistence on something other challenges our passive acceptance of a life of filling the vacant spaces left to us between work hours. **Art** challenges the identity we create through work and responsibilities to other people; it forces us to ask who we are when we stop doing these things so busily. **Art** encodes something of the vastness of the human mind and spirit, a vastness that mirrors that of the external world, of the night sky or the depths of the oceans. We can choose to engage with it, to allow our minds and spirits to resonate through it, or we can choose to fill the empty spaces of our life with game shows and TV shopping channels.

(Julian Johnson (*Who Needs Classical Music?: Cultural Choice and Musical Value*, Oxford: Oxford University Press, 2002, p.123))

Art is often ugly, usually difficult, sometimes boring. It doesn't care whether it pleases and indeed it would rather not. It refuses to give up its meaning without a fight, and insists that we work hard to make some sense of what is going on.

(Kathryn Hughes (*ER – Is it Art? Prospect* magazine, July 1999, p. 7))

Art – that difficult language of subtle symbols, resonating metaphors, poetic juxtapositions and unnatural structures which monkey about with time, space, logic. **Art** – which offers a view of the human condition that is not black and white but a spectrum of shades, a clash of colours, a mass of contradictions. **Art** – which blasphemously dissects and questions political, religious, and moral dogma; which reflects uncertainties; which is often years ahead of its time in the material it dares to handle and the structures within which it explores that material; which deals in levels of intellect and emotion the majority of people either cannot comprehend or do not wish to make the effort to comprehend.

(Arnold Wesker (The artist and the gatekeeper, *The Guardian*, 26 October 1992, p. 8))

Art, in other words, began to assume once again its age-old function as an agent of transformation, a method for making sense of the world, a vehicle for change at the level of consciousness, if not socio-political organisation.

(B. Ruby Rich (New times, *Sight and Sound*, August 1992))

The performing **arts** do more than entertain. They have a capacity to tell the truth, a value that cannot be measured in an accountant's report. It is through the **arts** (and sport) that we achieve some sense of collective identity. At a time when the country is suffering from a crisis of identity and a deep sense of moral uncertainty we need all the imaginative resources of our culture to articulate these issues and to help find a solution.

(Robert Hewison (The budget causes art attacks,
The Sunday Times, 5 December 1993, p. 25))

In listening to music, looking at art, reading poetry, going to plays we have the possibility of losing ourselves wholly in something outside ourselves – the most generous, the most cathartic of experiences. it can be of the same order of the giving of ourselves in sexual intercourse and the giving of ourselves involved in prayer, and is a purer activity than either, inasmuch as sex is always partly a mere relief of physiological pressures and prayer can be partly a form of insurance.

What is more aesthetic experience is something that can be shared by a substantial percentage of the human race, the illiterate as much as the educated ... Contemplation of objects from the past ... can provide spiritual nourishment that reaches our entrails, shapes our view of reality as a whole, our present awareness of life.

(David Sylvester (A fruitful loss of virginity,
The Guardian, 26 January 1994, p. 12))

Appendix 5
Credits for *The Dark Knight*

Warner Brothers (2008)

Directed by

Christopher Nolan

Writing:

Jonathan Nolan	(screenplay)
Christopher Nolan	(screenplay)
Christopher Nolan	(story)
David S. Goyer	(story)
Bob Kane	(characters)

Principal Cast:

Christian Bale	Bruce Wayne / Batman
Heath Ledger	The Joker
Aaron Eckhart	Dist. Atty. Harvey Dent / Two-Face
Michael Caine	Alfred
Maggie Gyllenhaal	Rachel Dawes
Gary Oldman	Gordon
Morgan Freeman	Lucius Fox
Monique Curnen	Det. Ramirez
Ron Dean	Detective Wuertz
Cillian Murphy	Scarecrow
Chin Han	Lau
Nestor Carbonell	Mayor Anthony Garcia
Eric Roberts	Salvatore Maroni
Ritchie Coster	The Chechen
Anthony Michael Hall	Mike Engel
Keith Szarabajka	Detective Stephens
Colin McFarlane	Commissioner Gillian B. Loeb
Joshua Harto	Coleman Reese
Melinda McGraw	Barbara Gordon
Nathan Gamble	James Gordon Jr.

Produced by

Kevin De La Noy	executive producer
Jordan Goldberg	associate producer
Philip Lee	line producer: Hong Kong
Karl McMillan	production associate producer
Benjamin Melniker	executive producer
Christopher Nolan	producer
Charles Roven	producer
Emma Thomas	producer
Thomas Tull	executive producer
Michael E. Uslan	executive producer

Original Music

James Newton Howard
Hans Zimmer

Cinematography

Wally Pfister

Film Editing

Lee Smith

Casting

John Papsidera

Production Design

Nathan Crowley

Supervising Art Direction

Simon Lamont

Set Decoration

Peter Lando

Costume Design

Lindy Hemming

Makeup Department Head

Peter Robb-King

Hair Department Head

Janice Alexander

Supervising Sound Editor

Richard King

Sound Designer

Richard King

Re-recording Mixers

Lora Hirschberg
Gari Rizzo

Sound Mixer

Ed Novick

Special Effects Supervisor

Chris Corbould

Notes

Introduction: cinema as entertainment

1 J. McCartney (2008) Our attitude to violence is beyond a joke, *The Sunday Telegraph*, July 27, p.17.
2 Rudolph Arnheim (1958) *Film as Art* (London: Faber and Faber). Bele Balazs (1952) *Theory of the Film* (London: Dennis Dobson). Ernest Lindgren (1955) *The Art of the Film* (London: Allen and Unwin).

1 What audiences go for

1 D. Docherty, D. Morrison, and M. Tracy (1987) *The Last Picture Show: Britain's Changing Film Audiences* (London: BFI).
2 R. Brustein (1959) The new Hollywood: myth and anti-myth, *Film Quarterly*, 12(3): 23–31.
3 T. Elsaesser (2005) *European Cinema: Face to Face with Hollywood* (Amsterdam: Amsterdam University Press), p. 300.
4 See Steven Powers, David J. Rothman and Stanley Rothman (1996) *Hollywood's America: Social and Political Themes in Motion Pictures* (Boulder, CO: Westview) for a fuller discussion of these issues.
5 Since there were only a handful of films that showed up in all lists, including the Foreign language group (i.e. films in which the language used is not English) used to balance out the results, the overall sample we investigated comprises of 146 films.
6 D. Bordwell, J. Staiger and K. Thompson (1985) *The Classical Hollywood Cinema: Film Style and Mode of Production to 1960* (New York: Columbia University Press); S. Field (1994) *Screenplay* (New York: Dell); R. McKee (1998) *Story* (London: Methuen).
7 1970 is, of course, a rough and ready marker of historical change.
8 Some films belong to more than one genre and this accounts for the seemingly odd results of having overall percentages that go over 100 per cent in total.
9 E. Peri (1961) Federico Fellini: an interview, *Film Quarterly*, 15(1): 30–3.
10 We do not wish to underestimate the importance of periodization but by indicating the contemporary period in Hollywood film-making as being post-*Jaws* we choose to follow what has proved perhaps the most enduring notion of periodization in Hollywood history, though this notion is problematized later in the chapter.
11 The data for the Critics list are even across the whole sample, with no specific clusters of films in either the original or adapted category in any given time period.
12 P. Kerr (2000) Starbucks and filthy Lucas, *The New Statesman*, 29 April, pp. 36–7.
13 For examples from each category, please refer to Appendix 1, p. 104.
14 A full explanation of this variable and its values is available in Appendix 1, p. 104.

15 M. C. Beltran (1995) The new Hollywood racelessness: only the fast, furious, (and multiracial) will survive, *Cinema Journal*, 44(2): 50–67.

16 We chose to focus on black characters as opposed to other ethnicities since it was the only coherent group represented in both lists, with the obvious exception of national races, e.g. a Japanese film would almost certainly feature Japanese characters.

17 Again, the figure would change somewhat if we had considered ethnicity with films like *The Godfather*, for instance.

18 Since 45 out of the 50 films in the Elite audience list were made prior to 1970, we felt it did not make statistical sense to analyse the difference in the presence of female or black protagonists in post-1970 films.

19 With such skewed results, we turned to the Foreign film list to check for consistency. This list showed a split not too dissimilar from the Mass list, with 46 per cent of films with a famous individual behind it and 54 per cent without.

20 In the absence of detailed statistical analysis and research, the figures published by the Motion Picture Association of America (MPAA) about movie-going habits in the US offer some interesting correlating data in this sense. The MPAA annual report can be accessed from the 'Research and Statistics' area of the MPAA website at http://www.mpaa.org/researchStatistics.asp. Also, the United States Census Bureau publishes all kind of statistics in relation to population make-up, income, race and other useful information. These resources can be accessed at: http://www.census.gov/

21 Meet Hollywood's latest genius, *Los Angeles Times*, 2 July 2006, section I, p. 16.

22 We believe that an argument could be built in order to answer Mlodinow's question. The extremely complex working situation of studio executives, with studios running constantly low on time and patience cannot possibly be conducive to highly sophisticated strategies. The production set-up of the studio era allowed greater planning powers to executives and producers, and certainly greater planning agility. Today the short life span of a top studio executive and the complexity of the film market conspire to create situations where decisions could easily be made for the short-term gain. Operational practices may thus provide a somewhat logical argument for not wanting to look at the long term and hence develop an allergy to learning lessons from historical trends and long-term data.

2 Sensual pleasure, audiences and *The Dark Knight*

1 P. E. Calderwood (2005) Risking aesthetic reading, *International Journal of Education & the Arts*, 6(3), available at: http://www.ijea.org/v6n3/v6n3.pdf

2 Discourses of sensual pleasure as 'lacking value', intended both in the sense of lacking moral gravity and in the sense of not being useful, are present in early writings on the arts, such as those of Aristotle, Socrates, and Cicero.

3 See, for instance, M. J. Adler (1937) *Art and Prudence: A Study in Practical Philosophy* (Adler Press, 2007 reprint).

4 For a useful recapitulation of the place of Kantian philosophy in the emergence of the notion of 'Art', see L. E. Shiner (2001) *The Invention of Art: A Cultural History* (Chicago: University of Chicago Press).

5   B. Vandenabeele (2001) On the notion of 'disinterestedness': Kant, Lyotard, and Scho-penhauer, *Journal of the History of Ideas*, 62(4): 705–20.

6   See I. Kant (2008) *The Critique of Judgement* (Oxford: Oxford University Press).

7   Aldous Huxley's (1932) novel *Brave New World* is perhaps one of the most exasperated version of these fears about cinema and technology in general.

8   D. Callaghan, The sensuality of cinema, interview for the Writers Guild of America, available at: http://www.wga.org/subpage.aspx?id=613

9   P. Bradshaw, The Dark Knight, *The Guardian*, 25 July, available at: http://www.guardian.co.uk/film/2008/jul/25/actionandadventure1

10 For a full discussion of the consequences of choosing to film some of the film in Imax and some in conventional 35mm, see D. Heuring (2008) The Dark Knight, *American Cinematographer*, 89(7), available at: http://www.ascmag.com/magazine_dynamic/July2008/The-DarkKnight/page1.php. For information on the Imax format, visit http://www.imax.com.

11 Ibid.

12 Ibid.

13 S. Brown (2008) Dark Knight director shuns digital effects for the real thing, *Wired*, 23 June, available at: http://www.wired.com/entertainment/hollywood/magazine/16-07/ff_darknight?currentPage=2.

14 It is truly remarkable that the city would allow Nolan and his collaborators to carry out incredible shots, such as the flipping of a 16-wheeler truck onto its head in the middle of Chicago's most famous street, LaSalle Street, as well as the blowing up of a very large building close to a main railroad and a network of roads.

15 D. Heuring, op. cit.

16 Ibid.

17 Ibid, available at: http://www.wired.com/entertainment/hollywood/magazine/16-07/ff_darknight?currentPage=3

18 This strategy is adopted for virtually all of the fight sequences where Batman is involved.

19 It is worth noting that a similar approach to the sound of Batman's voice seems to have partly backfired, as many critics and audience members have noted in articles and blogs about the film. For examples, see an anonymous press release from Associated Press reported by CNN, listing some of these comments from critics: What's with Batman's voice in 'Dark Knight'?, *Associated Press*, 4 August, available at: http://edition.cnn.com/2008/SHOWBIZ/Movies/08/04/mondaymoviebuzz.darkknight.ap/index.html

20 S. Dookey (2008) The Dark Knight original motion picture soundtrack review, *IGN*, 17 July, available at: http://uk.music.ign.com/articles/891/891639p1.html

21 D. Schweiger, CD Review: The Dark Knight, *Film Music Magazine*, 21 July, available at: http://www.filmmusicmag.com/?p=1736

22 S. Brown (2008), op. cit. available at: http://www.wired.com/entertainment/hollywood/magazine/16-07/ff_darknight?currentPage=4

23 Anonymous (2008) *Production Notes: The Dark Knight*, available from the official website of *The Dark Knight* at: http://thedarkknight.warnerbros.com in the 'About the Film' section of the site.

24 Ibid.

25 There are several instances of negative reviews, criticizing several different aspects of the film. See, for instance, articles and reviews in *The Wall Street Journal* ('What Bush and Batman have in common', available at: http://online.wsj.com/article/SB1216942473434

82821.html?mod=opinion_main_commentaries), in *The New York Observer* ('Bat to the future', available at: http://www.observer.com/2008/arts-culture/bat-future), in *The Daily Mail* ('Holy Moly! Batman's a big noise – but loses the plot', available at: http://www.dailymail.co.uk/tvshowbiz/reviews/article-1037123/Holy-Moly-Batmans-big-noise–loses-plot.html) and in widely read blogs, such as *The House Next Door* ('Trickster Heaven, two-faced Hell: The Dark Knight', available at: http://www.thehousenextdooronline.com/2008/07/trickster-heaven-two-faced-hell-dark.html).

3 Alfred Hitchcock

1   P. Wollen (1998) *Signs and Meaning in the Cinema* (London: British Film Institute), p. 38.
2   S. Bjorkman (ed.) (1994) *Woody Allen on Woody Allen* (London: Faber and Faber), p. 256.
3   S. Gottlieb (ed.) (1995) *Hitchcock on Hitchcock: Selected Writings and Interviews* (London: Faber and Faber), p. 126.
4   F. Truffaut (1969) *Hitchcock* (London: Panther), p. 278.
5   J. Rose (2001) *The Intellectual Life of the British Working Classes* (London: Yale University Press), p. 431.
6   Revealingly, in the early 1960s, when V.S. Pritchett was teaching in a Californian university, Hitchcock made contact and then consulted him extensively about the script of *The Birds*. Pritchett made a number of suggestions some of which were accepted and he even wrote (uncredited) some of the dialogue. One of Pritchett's stories was dramatized in the Hitchcock television series.
7   D. Spoto (1983) *The Dark Side of Genius* (London: Plexus), p. 135.
8   Hitchcock never seems to have had a substantial interest in politics. Patrick McGilligan says that, in the 1930s he shied away from taking political stands, even though the milieu he worked in was 'anti-fascist and socialist'. McGilligan also says that he never voted during his time in the USA. His attitude to politics in the post-war years seems to have been a mixture of the disengaged – he was an admirer of both Eisenhower and the Kennedys – and the conventional – he was anti-Soviet. There is almost no evidence of any response to the important political challenges of that period, the McCarthy witch hunts, the civil rights movement or the Vietnam War protests. P. McGilligan (2004) Alfred Hitchcock: *A Life in Darkness and Light* (New York: HarperCollins).
9   Gottlieb, op. cit., p. 57.
10   Spoto, op. cit., p. 406.
11   Gottlieb, op. cit., p. 37.
12   Ibid., p. 126.
13   Brian Moore, who wrote *Torn Curtain*, said, 'He had a preoccupation with the most trivial details of a story – such as what airline departs a city on a given day – but oddly, this was his strength at the time, and it assured a wealth of accurate historical and cultural and social detail.' However, Moore added that 'It also covered a profound ignorance of human motivation.'
14   Evan Hunter, who wrote the script of *The Birds*, discusses the impact of this on the making of the film in his book, *Me and Hitch*.
15   Patrick McGilligan reports that Hitchcock told Hayes that Kelly 'has a lot of charm and talent', 'but she goes through the motions as if she was in acting school. She does

everything properly and pleasantly, but nothing comes out of her. You've got to bring something out of her, bring her to life.'

16 David Badder, *Film Dope* 5, quoted in *The Internet Encyclopaedia of Cinematographers*, available at: http://www.cinematographers.nl/GreatDoPh/burks.htm

17 R. Allen and S. Ishi Gonzalès (1999) *Alfred Hitchcock Centenary Essays* (London: British Film Institute), pp. vii–viii.

18 A. Bazin (1954) Hitchcock v Hitchcock, in *Cahiers du Cinéma in English* (New York: Cahiers du Cinéma), p. 55.

19 Truffaut, op. cit., p. 398.

20 One of *Cahiers du Cinéma*'s innovations, the extended interview with directors, only made sense if you assume that what a director says about his/her film is meaningful.

21 L. Brill (1988) *The Hitchcock Romance* (Princeton, NJ: Princeton University Press), p. 19.

22 Spoto, op. cit., p. 392.

23 E. Lehman (1973) *North by Northwest* (London: Lorrimer), p. 12.

24 R. Wood (1965) *Hitchcock's Films* (London: Zwemmer), p. 99.

25 Jeff Millar in *The Houston Chronicle* quoted on *Rotten Tomatoes* website, available at: http://www.uk.rottentomatoes.com

26 D. Auiler (1999) *Vertigo: The Making of a Hitchcock Classic* (London: Titan Books), p. 161.

27 Hitchcock made a similar point in rather different terms. He felt James Stewart was too old for audiences to identify with the character he plays.

28 Although Hitchcock and most writers about the film tend to downplay the importance of the novel, the relationship between it and film is a close one. The plot and the main characters are taken without substantial alteration from *D'entre les morts*, as are many details such as lines of dialogue and colours (green is, for example, associated in the novel with moments of emotional intensity in the same way it is in the film). Some of the film's problems derive from the novel but so do some of its successes.

29 *Vertigo* script available on http://www.weeklyscript.com/Vertigo.txt

30 Ernst Lehman on *North by Northwest* DVD, London: Warner Home Video.

31 S. White (1999) *Vertigo* and problems of knowledge in feminist film theory in Richard Allen and S. Ishi Gonzalès, op. cit., p. 279.

4 Steven Spielberg, *Indiana Jones* and the Holocaust

1 L. Menaud (1998) Jerry don't surf, *New York Review of Books*, 24 September.

2 T. Shone (2004) *Blockbuster* (London: Scribner), p. 64.

3 J. McBride (1997) *Steven Spielberg* (London, Faber & Faber), p. 121.

4 L. Friedman and B. Notbohm (2000) *Steven Spielberg Interviews* (Jackson, MS: University Press of Mississippi), p. 112.

5 Ibid., p. 177.

6 P. Biskind (1999) *Easy Riders, Raging Bulls* (New York: Touchstone), p. 343.

7 Friedman and Notbohm, op. cit., p. 56.

8 McBride, op. cit., p. 122.

9 Ibid., p. 263.

10 S. Gould (1993) Dinomania, *New York Review of Books*, 12 August.

11 T. Stempel (2001) *American Audiences on Movies and Moviegoing* (Lexington, KY: University of Kentucky Press), p. 165.

12 J. Bobo (1995) *Black Women as Cultural Readers* (New York: Columbia University Press).

13 McBride, op. cit., p. 121.

14 Friedman and Notbohm, op. cit., p. 35.

15 Ibid., p. 27.

16 Ibid., p. 147.

17 Ibid., p. 116.

18 User comments on the *International Movie Database*, http://www.imdb.com

19 McBride, op. cit., p. 318.

20 Ibid., p. 313.

21 J. Gross (1994) Hollywood and the Holocaust, *New York Review of Books*, 3 February.

22 Ibid.

23 Y. Loshitzky (1997) *Spielberg's Holocaust: Critical Perspectives on Schindler's List* (Bloomington, IN: Indiana University Press), p. 80.

24 Friedman and Notbohm, op. cit., p. 163.

5 The perspective of entertainers

1 B. Frazer (2005) What Randy Thom hears: going deep in the mix with an Oscar-winning sound designer, *Film & Video*, 1 April, available at: http://www.studiodaily.com/filmandvideo/technique/craft/f/audio/4392.html

2 T. Kenny, *Walter Murch: The Search for Order in Sound & Picture*, available at: http://filmsound.org/murch/waltermurch.htm

3 Unless otherwise stated, all the interview material used in this chapter is from our own interviews with Thom and Murch. The interviews were carried out in March 2007 in Bolinas, CA, and at Skywalker Ranch, near San Rafael, CA.

4 For more information, visit the following websites. Zoetrope: http://www.zoetrope.com/; Lucasfilm: http://www.lucasfilm.com/; Pixar: http://www.pixar.com/. For the technologies mentioned, see the following sites: Dolby: http://www.dolby.com/; THX: http://www.thx.com/; Renderman: https://renderman.pixar.com/

5 Murch has won Oscars for his work on *Apocalypse Now* (1979) and *The English Patient* (1996). Thom has won Oscars for his work on *The Right Stuff* (1983) and *The Incredibles* (2004).

6 For full filmographies of both Murch and Thom, see Appendix 2 and Appendix 3.

7 For more information on Murch's father and his work, visit: http://www.winslowmyers.com/main.php?page=writings&page2=murch

8 USC is the abbreviation for the University of Southern California, Los Angeles, CA.

9 Interview with Randy Thom as part of NPR's celebration of WYSO, available at: http://www.npr.org/templates/story/story.php?storyId=11626209. WYSO still broadcasts today and can be accessed at: http://www.publicbroadcast.net/wyso/ppr/wyso.asx

10 KPFA continues to broadcast today and can be accessed at: http://157.22.130.4:8000/

11 Thomas Kincade interestingly refers to popular culture and Disney in particular as a major source of inspiration: 'Because I've nurtured my fantasy life since my youth, I am constantly aware of new influences and inspirations. I regularly seek out new places and

scenery as well as out of print books, comic books, obscure publications and even esoteric websites in search of imagery and ideas. One early form of inspiration came when as a young child I first visited Disneyland. I am convinced that Disneyland and the broader Disney vision shaped me in some defining way as a person and an artist.' http://tkpainteroflight.blogspot.com/ (posting entitled The Disney Collection, posted on Monday, 30 June 2008).

12 R. Thom, *On Being Creative – Reorganize Chance. That Is the Basis of Your Work*, originally published for CAS, *The Cinema Audio Society*, now available at: http://filmsound.org/randythom/creative.htm

13 M. Ondjaate (2002) *The Conversations: Walter Murch and the Art of Editing* (London: Bloomsbury), p.156.

14 J. Demme (1992) Demme on Demme, in J. Boorman and W. Donohoe *Projections No. 1* (London: Faber and Faber), p. 184.

15 P. Greengrass (2008) A whirlwind in action, *MediaGuardian*, 9 June, p. 5.

16 J. Hillier (1993) *The New Hollywood* (London: Studio Vista), p. 158.

17 D. Breskin (1997) *Inner Views: Filmmakers in Conversation* (New York: Da Capo Press), p. 162.

18 Ibid., p. 181.

19 S. Bjorkman (ed.) (1994) *Woody Allen on Woody Allen* (London: Faber and Faber), p. 103.

20 Ibid., p. 256.

21 Breskin, op. cit., p. 211.

22 Ibid., p. 220.

23 Ibid., p. 265.

24 N. Jordan (2005) The day the scales fell from my eyes, *The Guardian*, 14 May, p. 34.

25 J. Solomon (2006) We love Hidden. But what does it mean? *The Observer Review*, 19 February, p. 9.

26 Breskin, op. cit., p. 277.

27 J. Boorman and W. Donohoe (1999) *Projections No.10* (London: Faber and Faber), p. 117.

28 D. Puttnam (1997) The undeclared war, *The Guardian*, 9 May, p. 18.

29 Boorman and Donohoe, op. cit., p. 210.

30 R. Clark (ed.) (1986) *American Screenwriters* (Detroit: Gale Research Co.), p. 177.

31 Ibid., p. 274.

32 L. McMurtry (1987) *Film Flam* (New York: Touchstone), p. 67.

33 Clark, op. cit., p. 110.

34 Ibid., p. 92.

35 G. Fuller (1999) Getting out of his head, in J. Boorman and W. Donohoe *Projections No. 10* (London: Faber and Faber), p. 301.

6 The entertainment discourse

1 M. Litwak (1986) *Reel Power* (Los Angeles: Silman-James Press), p. 102.

2 Richard Dyer (1992) The notion of entertainment, in R. Dyer *Only Entertainment* (London: Routledge); R. Dyer, Entertainment and Utopia, in R. Dyer, ibid.; R. Maltby (2003) *Hollywood Cinema* (Oxford: Blackwell); S. Sayre and C. King (2003) *Entertainment & Society* (Fullerton: California State University), p. 2. There are other books whose titles promise a

response like *Studies in Entertainment: Studies in Mass Culture* (ed. Tania Modleski, 1986, Bloomington, IN: Indiana University Press) and *The Entertainment Functions of Television* (ed. Percy Tannenbaum, 1980, Hillsdale, NJ: Lawrence Erlbaum) but whose contributors take the word for granted and don't explore its meanings. And the same is true of many other books and articles in which the word is freely used.

3 Sayre and King, op. cit., p. 2.

4 R. Dyer (1992) *Only Entertainment* (London: Routledge), p. 18.

5 R. Maltby and I. Craven (1995) *Hollywood Cinema* (Oxford: Blackwell), p. 19.

6 J. Hillier (1993) *The New Hollywood* (London: Studio Vista), p. 150.

7 P. Preston (1999) Review of *Affliction, The Observer Review*, 21 February, p. 6.

8 A. McRobbie (1992) Mediocrity and delusion, *The Guardian*, 9 April, p. 8.

9 S. Makhmalbaf, *Iranian Cinema,* documentary transmitted on Channel 4, 10 May 2005.

10 W. Brooker and D. Jermyn (eds) (2003) *The Audience Studies Reader* (London: Routledge), p. 161.

11 S. O'Brien (1996) Awful truths in the thrills, *The Guardian*, 24 October, p. 10.

12 R. Denslow (2006) Incest, murder, abduction and fairies, *The Guardian*, films and music supplement, 20 January, p. 13.

13 R. Boston (1994) A cut above the sound and fury, *The Guardian*, 12 February, p. 6.

14 Joel Silver (1992) No ordinary Joel, *Empire Magazine*, September, p. 20.

15 F. Gibbons (2002) Unmade beds, pickled sharks, or just a can of worms? *The Guardian*, 1 November, p. 14.

16 R. Wood (1986) *Hollywood from Vietnam to Reagan* (Guildford: Columbia University Press), p. 78.

17 J. Rosenbaum (2000) *Movie Wars* (Chicago: A Cappella Books), p. 10.

18 J. Brewer (1997) *The Pleasures of the Imagination* (London: HarperCollins), p. 193.

19 S. de Beauvoir (1998) *America Day by Day* (London: Victor Gollancz), p. 340.

20 J. Radway (1991) *Reading the Romance* (Chapel Hill, NC: The University of North Carolina Press), p. 213.

21 And it is important to point out the small-scale nature of the book's research. It deals with one distinct literary genre and investigates the responses of fewer than 50 readers.

22 R. Putnam (2000) *Bowling Alone* (New York: Simon & Schuster), p. 230.

23 Ibid., p. 237.

24 A recent example is the government's announcement that it wanted schoolchildren to receive 5 hours of arts activities a week, despite all the other demands there are on the timetable.

25 C. Taylor (1989) *Sources of the Self* (Cambridge: Cambridge University Press), p. 422.

26 M. Woodmansee (1994) *The Author, Art, and the Market* (New York: Columbia University Press), p. 113.

27 Dyer, op. cit., p. 17.

28 S. Sontag (1996) 100 years of cinema, *The Guardian* Review, 2 March, p. 1. Our italics.

29 The discussion of Douglas Sirk's work that occurred in the 1970s provides another, more interesting, example of how these attitudes compromise the overall political position. From a left political perspective, critics began to celebrate the films Sirk directed in Hollywood in the late 1940s and 1950s, particularly those produced by Ross Hunter. On the face of it, films like *Magnificent Obsession, All That Heaven Allows, Written on the Wind* and *Imitation of Life* are perfect examples of what people mean when they talk about 'pure

entertainment' – wide screen, glossy, technicolour tearjerkers. Critics argued that, on the contrary, they were critical analyses which used the methods of self-reflexivity and distanciation to dissect bourgeois American society. If this is the case, some obvious questions arise about the responses of the original audiences. Did the audiences who saw the films when they were first shown recognize the critical attitude to the class system? If they didn't, what qualities of the films appealed to them, since they were very popular? The questions weren't even asked.

Barbara Klinger has quite rightly criticized this approach for neglecting what she calls 'the cathartic pleasures of soap opera'. She goes on to argue that by championing the films' social critique, and their use of self-reflexivity and distanciation, critics ignore the 'vulgar' enjoyment soap opera dramas offer. This approach divorces the critic from what Klinger calls, 'an image of a mindless, hedonistic crowd'. The damage such a view of the audience does to any position with left-wing pretensions is obvious.

Appendix 1

1   Box Office Mojo is available at: http://www.boxofficemojo.com (note: to access the full figures adjusted for inflation it is necessary to subscribe to Premier Pass). The Movie Times is available at: http://www.boxofficemojo.com. The Numbers is available at: http://www.the-numbers.com. Box Office Guru is available at: http://www.boxofficeguru.com/
2   The films are listed in the order of their ranking in the all-time, adjusted for inflation box-office as of 1 September 2007 from http://www.boxofficemojo.com
3   The full list can be accessed at: http://www.bfi.org.uk/sightandsound/topten/poll/critics-long.html
4   The films are listed in the order of their ranking in the BFI/Sight and Sound 2002 poll.
5   All data in this variable originated from the Academy Award official database, available at: http://www.oscars.org/awardsdatabase/

Annotated bibliography

We've listed below a selection of books and articles that have been particularly helpful to us in the writing of this book. We refer to some of them in our text (and details can be found in the notes). Others, although we don't refer to them directly, have stimulated and enlightened us. In one instance, Chapter 1: What audiences go for: elite and mass taste, we have written a separate appendix so please refer to that for the background to the chapter (Appendix 1).

2 Sensual pleasure, audiences and *The Dark Knight*

For general discussions of Kant and other philosophers' attitudes to sensual pleasure, we found M. J. Adler (1937) *Art and Prudence: A Study in Practical Philosophy* (New York: Adler Press) and B. Vandenabeele (2001) On the notion of 'disinterestedness': Kant, Lyotard, and Schopenhauer, *Journal of the History of Ideas*, 62(4): 705–20 of particular interest in that they discuss Kant's views at two different moments in time though reaching similar conclusions.

As for *The Dark Knight*, the film had just been released when we decided to write on it. As a consequence, most of the sources are either reviews in newspapers and magazines or viewers' own blogs and other websites. However, one very useful resource was provided by the production notes published on the official website for the film. They can be accessed by going to http://thedarkknight.com and then following links to the 'About the Film' section. The views expressed in the production notes come from virtually all of the key contributors to the film and are rather revealing of attitudes towards the film and its material.

A final note on P. E. Calderwood (2005) Risking aesthetic reading, *International Journal of Education & the Arts*, 6(3), available at: http://www.ijea.org/v6n3/v6n3.pdf . Although this piece is about literature and its sensual pleasures, we found it expressed views and sentiments close to our own and consequently we recommend it to anyone wishing to read on the same topic in relation to cinema.

3 Alfred Hitchcock: the entertainer becomes an artist

McGilligan and Spoto's biographies of Hitchcock both contain much useful background information. Spoto's book doesn't deserve to be dismissed simply because of its prurient interest in Hitchcock's sexual obsessions. It's informative and shows a good critical awareness of debates about Hitchcock's work.

Hitchcock at Work by Bill Krohn (London: Phaidon, 2003) and *Casting a Shadow: Creating the Alfred Hitchcock Film*, edited by Will Schmenner and Corinne Granoff

(Evanston, IL: North Western University Press, 2007) are helpful for their research into the making of Hitchcock's films. Both books demonstrate in detail how collaborative the process was. By doing this, they help to undermine the concept of the director as an individual, expressive artist. Sadly, against the grain of their research, both books try to hold on to established ideas about Hitchcock's genius.

Me and Hitch by Evan Hunter (London: Faber and Faber, 1997). Evan Hunter worked with Hitchcock on the scripts of both *The Birds* and *Marnie* (from which he was fired). This was the period when Hitchcock was becoming more fully aware of and sympathetic to the *Cahiers du Cinéma* celebration of him as a great artist. Hunter describes well some of the consequences this had on Hitchcock's approach to his work.

4 Steven Spielberg, *Indiana Jones* and the Holocaust

Like Spoto's and McGilligan's biographies of Hitchcock, Joseph McBride's biography of Spielberg contains much useful information. It's also good at setting Spielberg's work in the context of late twentieth-century Hollywood cinema.

The best overall critical account of Spielberg's work we've come across is Stephen Rowley's article on the Senses of Cinema website (www.sensesofcinema.com)

Alice Walker's account of the making of *The Color Purple* in her book, *The Same River Twice – Honoring the Difficult* (London: Phoenix, 2005) describes in a generous way the challenges that Spielberg faced in turning her novel into a film. Her description highlights the collective nature of film-making and is particularly helpful for its discussion of the black audience response to the film.

5 Film-makers as entertainers? Interviews with Randy Thom and Walter Murch

The vast majority of the chapter is taken from original interviews that we carried out in Spring 2007 in California. Wherever possible, we augmented these with other significant extracts from interviews from other sources. In this sense, the best resource for anyone wishing to learn more about Murch's and/or Thom's views is the special sections dedicated to the two film-makers available at http://www.filmsound.org.

There is a wide variety of sources for the views of other film-makers. The best of those sources are the interviews in D. Breskin (1997) *Inner Views: Filmmakers in Conversation* (New York: Da Capo Press) and are particularly valuable because they are sustained and extensive. The *Projections* series, published by Faber and Faber in the UK, is another particularly helpful source.

Our own book, A. Lovell and G. Sergei (2005) *Making Films in Contemporary Hollywood* (London: Hodder) also contains a fuller listing of relevant sources.

6 The entertainment discourse

The Pleasures of the Imagination: English Culture in the Eighteenth Century by John Brewer (London: HarperCollins, 1997). Brewer's book is a beautifully produced and illuminating account of English culture at a time when many of the issues that are central today, especially pleasure and the nature of the arts, first began to be questioned.

What Good are the Arts? by John Carey (London: Faber & Faber, 2005). In the main part of his book, John Carey convincingly undermines the main arguments that are advanced to justify the importance of the arts. However, the last part of the book demonstrates the power of the belief in the value of the arts. In it, Carey goes against the thrust of his previous argument and tried to demonstrate that his art, literature, does have value.

The Author, Art, and the Market by Martha Woodmansee (New York: Columbia University Press, 1994). Since it centres on debates about literature and culture in eighteenth-century Germany, Martha Woodmansee's book might seem remote from the concerns of this book. But her discussion of the debates is as suggestive and illuminating as John Brewer's discussion of the English debates. Of particular value is the way she relates those debates to the economic and social changes of the period.

The Amusements of the People, two essays by Charles Dickens in *The Uncollected Writings of Charles Dickens: Household works, 1850–1859*, edited with an introduction and notes by Harry Stone, Vol. 1 (London: Allen Lane, 1969). Dickens' two essays about the London theatre are models of their kind. They express sympathetic, engaged attitudes towards popular entertainment and are noteworthy for their detailed attention to the character and responses of audiences.

Dickens's Villains: Melodrama, Character, Popular Culture by Juliet John (Oxford: Oxford University Press, 2001). Juliet John provides a helpful guide to Dickens' attitude to popular entertainment and makes helpful connections with contemporary debates about culture and politics.

Sources of the Self: The Making of Modern Identity by Charles Taylor (Cambridge, MA: Harvard University Press, 1989). As the subtitle suggests, Charles Taylor's opus is principally concerned with the nature of modern identity. Along the way, his discussion of how concepts of art relate illuminates how art is conceived in contemporary cultural discussion.

Note that all websites listed in the book were checked for consistency on 1 August 2008. Consequently, we have not added to our reference notes the traditional 'last accessed'.

Index

RETHINKING DOCUMENTARY
New Perspectives and Practices

Thomas Austin and Wilma de Jong

From a boom in theatrical features to footage posted on websites such as *YouTube* and *Google Video*, the early years of the 21st century have witnessed significant changes in the technological, commercial, aesthetic, political, and social dimensions of documentaries on film, television and the web.

In response to these rapid developments, this book rethinks the notion of documentary, in terms of theory, practice and object/s of study. Drawing together 26 original essays from scholars and practitioners, it critically assesses ideas and constructions of documentary and, where necessary, proposes new tools and arguments with which to examine this complex and shifting terrain.

Covering a range of media output, the book is divided into four sections:

- Critical perspectives on documentary forms and concepts
- The changing faces of documentary production Contemporary documentary: borders, neighbours and disputed territories
- Digital and online documentaries: opportunities and limitations

Rethinking Documentary is valuable reading for scholars and students working in documentary theory and practice, film studies, and media studies.

Contents: *Part 1: Critical perspectives on documentary forms and concepts – John Corner – Bill Nichols – Michael Renov – Thomas Austin – Silke Panse – Mike Wayne – Paul Basu – Erik Knudsen – Michael Chanan – Part 2: The changing faces of documentary production – Wilma de Jong – Jerry Rothwell – Marilyn Gaunt – An interview with John Smithson by Wilma de Jong and Thomas Austin – An interview with Ralph Lee by Wilma de Jong – Ishmahil Blagrove, Jr – An interview with Ai Xiaoming by Sue Thornham – Part 3: Contemporary documentary: borders, neighbours and disputed territories – Paul Ward – Craig Hight – Annette Hill – Su Holmes and Deborah Jermyn – Jon Dovey – Nick Couldry and Jo Littler – Part 4: Digital and online documentaries: opportunities and limitations – Ana Vicente – Danny Birchall – Patricia R. Zimmermann – Alexandra Juhasz.*

2008 376pp

978-0-335-22191-2 (Paperback) 978-0-335-22192-9 (Hardback)

THE BOLLYWOOD READER

Rajinder Dudrah and Jigna Desai (eds)

"From its historical roots through to the contemporary moment, the collection of essays, written by eminent scholars in the field, demonstrate so clearly how Indian cinema is more than the sum of its parts. An essential text for anyone wishing to understand properly the full complexities of Hindi cinema."

Professor Susan Hayward, University of Exeter, UK

"We are finally at a point when the study of Bollywood is a fully fledged field in Film Studies."

Professor Dina Iordanova, University of St. Andrews, Scotland

"The Bollywood Reader extends the discursive boundaries of Indian popular cinema in interesting and complex ways. In putting together this volume, the editors have performed magnificently."

Professor Wimal Dissanayake, University of Hawaii, USA

- What is Bollywood cinema?
- How does it operate as an industry?
- Who are the audiences of Bollywood cinema?

These are just some of the questions addressed in this lively and fascinating guide to the cultural, social and political significance of popular Hindi cinema, which outlines the history and structure of the Bombay film industry, and its impact on global popular culture.

Including a wide-ranging selection of essays from key voices in the field, the Reader charts the development of the scholarship on popular Hindi cinema, with an emphasis on understanding the relationship between cinema and colonialism, nationalism, and globalization. Features include:

- Comprehensive introductory essay
- Landmark essays by key scholars in the field
- Glossary of key terms
- Timeline of key events in Indian cinema
- Further reading section

The authors address the issues of capitalism, nationalism, Orientalism and modernity through understandings of race, class, gender and sexuality, religion, politics and diaspora as depicted in Indian popular films.

The Bollywood Reader is captivating reading for film, media and cultural studies students and scholars with an interest in Bollywood cinema.

Contents: *List of contributors – Acknowledgements – Publisher's acknowledgements – Part 1 Theoretical frameworks – Part 2 Recent trajectories – Part 3 Bollywood abroad and beyond – Select keywords – Select timeline – Further reading – Index.*

2008 384pp

978-0-335-22212-4 (Paperback) 978-0-335-22213-1 (Hardback)

THE CULT FILM READER

Ernest Mathijs and Xavier Mendik (eds)

"A really impressive and comprehensive collection of the key writings in the field. The editors have done a terrific job in drawing together the various traditions and providing a clear sense of this rich and rewarding scholarly terrain. This collection is as wild and diverse as the films that it covers. Fascinating."

> Mark Jancovich, Professor of Film and Television Studies, University of East Anglia, UK

"It's about time the lunatic fans and loyal theorists of cult movies were treated to a book they can call their own. The effort and knowledge contained in The Cult Film Reader will satisfy even the most ravenous zombie's desire for detail and insight. This book will gnaw, scratch and infect you just like the cult films themselves."

> Brett Sullivan, Director of Ginger Snaps Unleashed and The Chair

"The Cult Film Reader is a great film text book and a fun read."

> John Landis, Director of The Blues Brothers, An American Werewolf in London and Michael Jackson's Thriller

Whether defined by horror, kung-fu, sci-fi, sexploitation, kitsch musical or 'weird world cinema', cult movies and their global followings are emerging as a distinct subject of film and media theory, dedicated to dissecting the world's unruliest images.

This book is the world's first reader on cult film. It brings together key works in the field on the structure, form, status, and reception of cult cinema traditions. Including work from key established scholars in the field such as Umberto Eco, Janet Staiger, Jeffrey Sconce, Henry Jenkins, and Barry Keith Grant, as well as new perspectives on the gradually developing canon of cult cinema, the book not only presents an overview of ways in which cult cinema can be approached, it also re-assesses the methods used to study the cult text and its audiences.

With editors' introductions to the volume and to each section, the book is divided into four clear thematic areas of study – The Conceptions of Cult; Cult Case Studies; National and International Cults; and Cult Consumption – to provide an accessible overview of the topic. It also contains an extensive bibliography for further related readings.

Written in a lively and accessible style, *The Cult Film Reader* dissects some of biggest trends, icons, auteurs and periods of global cult film production. Films discussed include *Casablanca*, *The Rocky Horror Picture Show*, *Eraserhead*, *The Texas Chainsaw Massacre*, *Showgirls* and *Ginger Snaps*.

Essays by: *Jinsoo An; Jane Arthurs; Bruce Austin; Martin Barker; Walter Benjamin; Harry Benshoff; Pierre Bourdieu; Noel Carroll; Steve Chibnall; Umberto Eco; Nezih Erdogan; Welch Everman; John Fiske; Barry Keith Grant ; Joan Hawkins; Gary Hentzi; Matt Hills; Ramaswami Harindranath; J.Hoberman; Leon Hunt; I.Q. Hunter; Mark Jancovich; Henry Jenkins; Anne Jerslev; Siegfried Kracauer; Gina Marchetti; Tom Mes; Gary Needham; Sheila J. Nayar; Annalee Newitz; Lawrence O'Toole; Harry Allan Potamkin; Jonathan Rosenbaum; Andrew Ross; David Sanjek; Eric Schaefer; Steven Jay Schneider; Jeffrey Sconce; Janet Staiger; J.P. Telotte; Parker Tyler; Jean Vigo; Harmony Wu*

Contents: *Section One: The Concepts of Cult – Section Two: Cult Case Studies – Section Three: National and International Cults – Bibliography of Cult Film Resources – Index.*

2007 576pp

978-0-335-21923-0 (Paperback) 978-0-335-21924-7 (Hardback)